UNLIMITED:

Conquering the Myth of the Glass Ceiling

UNLIMITED:

Conquering the Myth of the Glass Ceiling

Cortney D. Baker, Ed. D.

Clovercroft Publishing

Unlimited: Conquering the Myth of the Glass Ceiling

©2017 by Cortney D. Baker

Published by Clovercroft Publishing, Franklin, Tennessee
Edited by Christine Messier
Cover Design by Stan Hulen
Interior Design by Suzanne Lawing

ISBN: 978-1-945507-20-5

Printed in the United States of America

Contents

INTRODUCTION

Ladies, We Have a Problem

By the ripe old age of thirty-seven, I'd already worked myself out of a job. I owned my own pediatric home healthcare company, KidsCare Therapy, in Dallas, Texas, since 2003, but had been actively moving into a more supportive role in the business for quite some time. As such, I transitioned into CEO and Chairman of the Board for KidsCare, but wasn't needed on a daily basis.

Having the time and ability to do it, I decided to fulfill a dream of mine to further my education. After looking around for the best program to attend, I landed on one that had exactly what I wanted; in August 2012, I started my doctoral journey in organizational leadership at Pepperdine University.

When two-and-a-half years of course work, national and international consulting trips, and comprehensive exams were finished, I rolled up my sleeves and mentally prepared to tackle the dreaded dissertation. It made the most sense to study something familiar to me—after all, the best dissertation is a done dissertation (and I figured studying something I cared about would make the process more palatable).

Because of my background as a speech-language pathologist, I decided to study women leaders in healthcare. A bit broad, right? So I asked myself, "What did I want to find out? What's the burning question that keeps me up at night?" There were so many avenues I could pursue, but I needed to stay focused. I needed to identify one central question that intrigued me enough to dedicate my dissertation, time, devotion, and life (and some would argue my sanity, but that's another story) to finding the answer.

Problem: Not Just Healthcare

I dove into current literature and discovered women make up approximately 51 percent of the United States population—so technically, albeit slightly, we're the gender majority, ladies. We also hold about 46.8 percent of the jobs that contribute to the American labor force (Catalyst, 2016). In our employment roles, we reportedly hold approximately 52 percent of mid-level manager, professional, and related positions.

So, let's get this straight: in the U.S., *women are half the population, we hold about half the jobs, and we make up about half the labor pool of mid-level management.* Obviously, we're making some significant headway in the workforce toward gender equality, right? Wrong. When it comes to the highest paid position of chief executive officers of S&P 500 companies, women hold only 20 positions, or 4 percent, of those roles. *On the 2016 Fortune 500 list, only 4.2 percent of the companies had women employed as CEOs.*

Do you see anything wrong with those numbers? I certainly did. According to the data, across every American industry, women contribute to all levels of organizational productivity and profitability, as we've been successful in climbing to the mid-level ranks of corporate leadership. However, it quickly became evident to me that something has been keeping women from obtaining the highest tier of employment positions in corporate America.

Although we hold nearly 52 percent of all professional-level positions, we substantially lag behind men when it comes to employment and representation in executive-level positions. In fact, here's a summary of some interesting data and figures regarding American women in leadership (Warner, 2014):

- Women's presence in top management positions remains below 9 percent.

- Women earn nearly 60 percent of undergraduate and master's degrees.

- Women earn 48 percent of all medical degrees and 47 percent of all law degrees.

- Women are 47 percent of the workforce and comprise nearly 60 percent of the college-educated workforce—at the entry level.

- In the legal field, women are 45.4 percent of associates, but make up only 25 percent of non-equity partners and 15 percent of equity partners.

- In the financial services industry, women are 54 percent of the labor pool, but are only 12.4 percent of executive officers, and 18 percent of board directors, and none are CEOs.

- In the medical industry, women are 34.3 percent of physicians and surgeons but less than 16 percent of medical school deans.

- Women control 80 percent of consumer spending in the American economy, but they comprise only 3 percent of advertising's creative directors.

I'm sure current social media and news coverage have already brought this subject to your attention. However, there's more to the continued gender disparity than just the female glass ceiling, and I quickly realized the healthcare industry is no different.

When digging through the data, I discovered the healthcare industry is comprised of 75-80 percent female employees (U.S. Department of Labor, Bureau of Labor Statistics, 2015). That made complete sense when I considered the landscape of those in the field: nurses, nurse assistants, nurse practitioners, therapists, physicians, physician assistants, etc.

However, when it came to healthcare leadership positions, I found that only about 11 percent of CEOs are female, and that number has been stable for decades (American College of Healthcare Executives (ACHE), 2012). I was appalled by the low percentage of women in leadership positions in the industry, and I began to question why.

If the talent pool is predominantly female, where are all the female leaders?

As a female CEO of a healthcare organization, I wanted to know where all my female peers were, and specifically, what was keeping women from leadership opportunities in our industry? What challenges and obstacles do women face when advancing their careers? Aha! That was my research question!

I wanted to hear from women who'd successfully climbed the healthcare corporate ladder and understand what experiences they'd endured in order to obtain C-level positions. The research indicated that just over 10 percent of women successfully navigated through the corporate ranks of the female-dominated world of healthcare, but that statistic wasn't high enough to satisfy me. Women had barely broken the double-digit mark in executive-level leadership and that was just not good enough. Despite the belief that women shattered the glass ceiling long ago, a large, noticeable absence of females among the executive-level healthcare positions remained (McDonagh & Paris, 2013).

I thought if we, as a gender, could identify what was standing in our way of achieving executive positions, we could finally move beyond the challenges of being the only female in the boardroom. We could stand together as a group with a common goal to collectively pave the way for a more diverse leadership landscape for those who'd come behind us and follow our lead. I was thrilled to know I'd finally discover and expose the injustice of what was hindering female leaders from finding their rightful place in executive-level ranks of the healthcare world; but first, I had to do the research.

My goal was to identify what challenges and obstacles women experience and overcome in their healthcare career journeys. For my dissertation research, I interviewed ten females who'd successfully navigated the corporate ladder and obtained C-level positions. My participants ranged from chief executive officers, chief development officer, chief financial officers, chief medical officers, and chief nursing officers, and they were located all over the United States.

In order to obtain their perspectives on the challenges they faced, I asked each of them seven questions. I heard rich, detailed stories of how they worked their way beyond the proverbial glass ceiling and were able to obtain positions in what I believed were considered the "coveted" corner offices. However, upon hearing their stories, I quickly realized earning those positions hadn't been easy.

The women spoke candidly of their differing journeys, but one common thread was evident: they all shared stories of struggle and perseverance, which brought up reflections and stories of my personal experiences when starting my company. Each participant charted her own unique course, but the findings of the research determined that these women experienced and overcame four main challenges and obstacles to gain their respective roles.

Although my original research was limited to these women, my quest to uncover the truth of the problems was just beginning. I furthered my research by reading everything I could get my hands on, while continuing the conversation with more women. I informally interviewed women all over the country in various positions and industries, and found the four challenges and obstacles we face appear to be universal and widespread.

Of all the women I interviewed, the reported challenges and obstacles were similar to one another. Not everyone spoke of experiencing all four challenges, but every woman I talked to dealt with some combination of them.

Conquering the Myth of the Glass Ceiling

My intent in writing this book is to share the findings of the research, so you'll know you aren't alone in the journey. Other women have experienced, and are continuing to face, the same obstacles when advancing their careers. However, I didn't want to only talk about the problems, because what's the good in that? I also offer suggestions and solutions for any woman who resonates with these common challenges and hurdles. I hope you consider this book your personal guide to navigating your career path. Think of it as your roadmap to your career.

You see, I believe the glass ceiling doesn't exist. It's a myth we've believed for years, which has contributed to our lack of progress. Now hear me out, before you get mad and throw this book across the room! Don't get me wrong; I'm completely aware (and in agreement) the conventional ladder of career advancement hasn't been favorable for women's promotions and advancements. That's been repeatedly proven through various studies over the years.

I'm not saying the glass ceiling isn't something that wasn't real in the past, because those who went before us encountered blatant gender discrimination in the workforce. And thankfully women like Susan B. Anthony, Ida B. Wells, Dorothy Height, and Elizabeth Cady Stanton worked very hard to fight for the laws and tides of equality to begin turning. And I'm not saying some of you aren't experiencing blatant gender discrimination now, because that's a very real possibility.

A New Perspective

The whole point of a maze is to persevere at every twist and turn until you reach the end goal.

But, I believe we must consider our barriers to be penetrable and surmountable. Think about it: a ceiling, by design, is an obstruction not intended to be penetrated—there's no reason to break through it. Why would you want to, anyway? And the fact that the ceiling is referred to as glass insinuates that it's an invisible barrier. Therefore, by buying into the myth of the glass ceiling means that we are fighting invisible challenges that aren't meant to be won.

On the other hand, if we look at our struggles and challenges as a labyrinth or maze, our perspective changes. The whole point of a maze is to persevere at every twist and turn until you reach the end, knowing there will be times where we hit dead-ends, bumps in the road, and unsure paths. However, when we know what we're facing we can arm ourselves to pursue the journey, to persevere and succeed to the end.

And in this case, our end would be higher-level leadership positions through career advancement. Instead, if we look at our career journeys through a slightly different lens, then we have the chance, the amazing opportunity, to be successful—to CONQUER!

My dream is that we all begin to look at our journeys through the eyes of a kindred tribe, banded together to conquer the executive level. That's certainly better than seeing ourselves as solitary victims walking our paths alone and believing it's every "man" for himself against an imaginary obstacle destined to keep us down. Our goal now shouldn't be to break through a glass ceiling, but to persevere and overcome the challenges that inevitably lie in front of us, and triumph.

I'm confident we hold the keys to unlocking the doors of the corner offices, if we so choose. The empowering part is that the answers lie within us. Therefore, I encourage you to get your favorite pair of shoes on, because you're about to walk the road to conquering career success.

But first: Ladies, we have some problems. So let's get started—together!

PART ONE
History Plays a Role

In the working world, women are accomplishing more than ever before—serving in the military, fighting crime, running companies, leading research teams, and so much more. In every year since 2008, women have earned the majority of doctoral degrees, and in graduate schools in 2014, women outnumbered men 136 to 100 (Perry, 2015). We're employed in positions and breaking ground in areas once reigned solely by men.

It would be nice to think that our battles of workplace equality have been won, but that's simply not the case. Our reality is this: in the American workforce we've come a long way, but we still have a long road ahead of us. American men continue to hold most of the corporate leadership positions, with women holding less than 15 percent of executive officer roles (Warner, 2014).

Although keenly aware of the battle for boardroom equality, I found my research ignited an internal fire I didn't know I had. I'd come across a troubling statistic about women in healthcare that made my blood boil—not only did the gender disparity still exist, but the research stated that little had been done to narrow the gap since the study was first conducted in 1990 (American College of Healthcare Executives, 2012).

Seriously…1990? Twenty-seven years without significant change? Are you kidding me? Although that statistic was specific to healthcare, I had a sneaking suspicion I'd find similar data and stories of the perpetuation of gender disparity, regardless of the industry.

I was ready to begin my journey of digging into the research and interviewing participants, in order to get to the bottom of what was holding women back from the upper ranks of leadership. Once the interviews for my doctoral research were concluded, I furthered my findings by talking to many other women in different industries. Story after story affirmed my suspicions—women indicated that the challenges we deal with aren't industry-specific; they are, however, gender-specific.

Over the next several chapters, we'll examine the obstacles experienced by the participants, along with strategies and suggestions to assist in overcoming these struggles. The first challenge the women identified was pretty obvious, in my opinion. The other three were quite surprising.

CHAPTER 1

Balancing Family and Career

Life is about balance, and we all have to make the effort in areas that we can to enable us to make a difference.

~ ORLANDO BLOOM

Of the four challenges we face as women when growing our careers, which one do you think also has the power to bring us immense stress, but also love, joy, and fulfillment? Ah, yes, of course…the youngsters.

The first obstacle identified was that balancing a family with the demands of an advancing career continues to be a source of struggle for professional women. This conflict is partially the result of the historic role women have taken when it comes to the home and family responsibilities, especially with respect to raising children. I'm sure you're thinking, "Tell me something I don't know, genius."

But seriously, even in the 21st century women continue to remain responsible for the largest portion of home responsibilities and caretaking of others. Working women are typically CEOs of their home: organizing family activities, healthcare appointments, cooking, cleaning, soccer practice, grocery shopping, laundry, etc. According to a 2014 article in the *New York Times*, "women are not equally represented at the top of corporate America because of the basic facts of motherhood:

Even the most ambitious women scale back at work to spend more time on child care. At least, that's the conventional wisdom" (Miller, 2014). Ultimately, women experience more time commitments between their personal and professional lives than their male counterparts. This challenge is of greatest magnitude for women when trying to raise a family while navigating professional careers, regardless of where they fall on the career ladder (Eagly & Carli, Through the labyrinth: The truth about how women become leaders, 2007).

Working women are typically CEOs of their home.

In the U.S., about 60 percent of the homes made up of married families with children have both parents employed in the labor force (U.S. Census Bureau, 2013). That doesn't even account for the growing number of homes that have single-parent families, with that number rising to 12 million in 2015; nearly 84 percent of those are led by single mothers (U.S. Census Bureau, 2015).

I've been a single mom. I know the struggle and difficulty of trying to balance it all and keep everything moving in the right direction when you don't even know in what direction you're supposed to be going. It's hard. It's a challenge. But it can be done.

I'll never forget when I was a single mom finishing the spring semester of my last year of graduate school in Illinois, where my six-year-old son and I lived. All of our family lived in Texas, easily a ten-hour car ride away. Because of my schedule and internship placement, I had to intern at a private school during the day and work at my graduate assistantship at the university in the evening. I worked until eight or nine o'clock four nights a week.

In order to get all my hours in so I could graduate on time, I enrolled my first-grade son in evening 'daycare.' He took the bus from school to the childcare facility, and I picked him up after my work shift at night. Not seeing him for what was basically an entire semester wasn't an ideal situation, but I looked at it as a means to an end. I knew it wouldn't last forever, and it didn't. It was the only way I could manage it all. If you're a single mom, my hat goes off to you. Keep up the good work; I know it feels like your hard work goes unnoticed, but you're showing your children a resilience and strength they'll never forget.

For married women with children, according to time diary studies, for every one hour per week males devoted to household responsibilities, females reportedly spent 1.7 hours, nearly twice that of men, during the same time duration. Although home duties are now more evenly distributed than they've been during any other previous time in history, a striking difference still remains between men and women's time spent on domestic chores.

Women are generally responsible for essential activities, such as cleaning, cooking, and laundry; while men typically do home maintenance tasks, yard work, and paying the bills. The duties women are in charge of are more repetitive, frequent, and harder to skip, with the inflexibility of the demands adding to their load.

Mothers also provide more direct childcare than fathers, with married women performing double the amount of care that fathers do (Eagly & Carli, 2007a). However, it's important to acknowledge that in America both parents spend more time engaging with their children than previous generations.

Despite the fact that males are engaging more often in domestic responsibilities and child-rearing, these contributors still affect women and their access to authority and power in the workplace and community (Eagly & Carli, 2007a). As a result, female executives face more difficulties in juggling career and family needs than their male counterparts.

Marriage, and especially having children, typically places differing demands on women than men. Females in professional and managerial roles generally have the most intense time struggles between balancing their family duties and their job, as a result of the long hours their employment requires (American College of Healthcare Executives, 2012; Eagly & Carli, 2007a). Work demands—such as emails, phone calls, or possibly night and/or weekend shifts—often infringe on personal lives. Many women have job obligations and responsibilities that come into conflict with their family requirements and schedules.

So what gets compromised when working mothers try to balance it all? Not surprisingly, it's Mom. Women generally compensate for their hours spent away from home by forgoing free time and personal activities to spend time with their children. The more time Mom puts in at work, the less time she spends in social or leisure capacities. A woman's recreation time is reduced by an hour a day when she is married or has a child under the age of six; yet marriage or children does not affect a man's leisure and relaxation time (Eagly & Carli, 2007a).

The demands between family and employment never cease, causing women to feel more hurried and pressed for time than men. As a result, some women have less consistent and continuous employment, in turn allowing for fewer opportunities for career advancement among professional ranks (Eagly & Carli, 2007a).

A woman's recreation time is reduced by an hour a day when she is married or has a child under the age of six.

A considerable number of women make the determination to set aside time for family duties altogether by resigning their careers completely. A 2005 study found that 37 percent of women who obtained either their undergraduate degree with honors, professional, or graduate degrees voluntarily resigned from their employment at some point in their careers (as opposed to a reported 24 percent of men).

For mothers with one or more children, that number grew to 43 percent. When asked, the main reason females reported they took time away from their careers was to allocate time to the family; men, however, reported that their leave of absence was to switch careers (Hewlett & Luce, 2005).

Frequently, females' crucial years for working hard toward growing and establishing favorable careers coincide with their prime years for bearing children, often making the cost of suspending employment even worse. In some cases, women make the detrimental decision to halt their employment prior to ever attempting to advance it. They consider their current earnings, position, and work status and resolve to leave the workforce to devote time to growing their families and raising their children.

However, often what they fail to consider is the potential for advancement they'd have in their careers if they chose to move up in positions as opposed to checking out. All too often women are told they have to make the choice between family and career, because attempting to do both—and do them both well—is difficult at best, and impossible at worst.

Most people, male and female, undeniably agree that raising children is one of the hardest and most important jobs a person can have. Why is it, then, that women who take time to devote to this often thankless effort are most often met with closed doors to the corporate world when they try to reenter the employment market? Even for females with exceptional educational credentials, it can take hard work to regain career momentum (Eagly & Carli, 2007a).

Is that because women are choosing to stay home and not work? Not necessarily, although only about 74 percent of female professionals will return to employment outside the home in any capacity; and only 40 percent will rejoin the workforce in a full-time position. Interestingly, though, many women stated they would consider working again—if the conditions were right.

> *Many women stated they would consider working again—*
> *if the conditions were right.*

Of course, not all of the women I spoke with had children, and many of those made a conscious decision not to. Ann, a hospital CEO, stated she was committed to her career and early on had the deliberate conversation with her husband that they would not attempt to further their family by adding children to the mix due to the demands of her career path.

But of the female participants in both formal and informal interviews, every woman who was a parent spoke of the family responsibilities and commitments as being among the biggest challenges she encountered while attempting to advance her career. Many discussed the desire for more balance between their two worlds, but had no suggestions or ideas on how to achieve their desired equilibrium. Due to whatever stage of life the women were in, the challenge of balancing family with a career differed depending on the ages of the child(ren).

What complicated this problem was the perceived lack of support they felt, often in both worlds. Some reported that family members, friends, or acquaintances said hurtful things regarding being employed outside the home. "My mother-in-law is the worst when it comes to making remarks about me working. She constantly makes snide comments insinuating that my kids don't even know me. What's hardest is she had the ability to be a stay-at-home mom, but we don't have that opportunity. The thing is, I like to work. I genuinely like having adult conversations in a stimulating environment. I like the sense of accomplishment I feel, but I also feel guilty," one contributor said.

Another participant spoke of recently being approached at a party by a friend's father, who asked her if she was still working. "I just stood there in amazement that he would even think to ask me that. I mean, it's not like he'd walk up to my husband and ask that same question. Why did he think it was okay to ask me? Is he just expecting me to quit my job because we have three kids?"

Another area in which professional women reported experiencing similar challenges was in dealing with comments or actions of other non-working or part-time working women. Many of the women discussed feeling judged or felt women who were able to help with school and afterschool activities more often were questioning their parenting skills and abilities.

One contributor, Sara, stated, "I was at my son's kindergarten Christmas party and all of the other moms were there. The majority of them don't work outside the home, or if they do, they work part-time. That was the first party I'd been able to attend for the year because of my schedule, and I felt bad that I hadn't helped. So I told the room mom that I would be happy to do something for the end of the year party, if she needed it.

"She just looked me up and down, like so many women seem to do, and sort of laughed and said in a very sarcastic tone that she was sure I was too busy to worry about such a small thing and that she and the other room moms had everything under control. I was so upset. My face was burning and all I wanted to do was leave, but my son was so happy to have me there. I tried to focus on that instead of the fact that I felt like all eyes were on me."

That, my friends, would not have ended well if I had been there. I can't imagine how I would have responded in that situation, but I assure you I would have needed my filter on for it to be socially appropriate for a kindergarten party. Why is it that some people get enjoyment out of being hateful to others? Well, that's another conversation we'll address later.

CHAPTER 2

Always on Call

Whatever your calling, the real test of your career longevity will come during the valleys. How will you rally and pick yourself up during those downtimes?

~ CAROL LEIFER

The third area women reported experiencing complications balancing family responsibilities and a professional career was at their place of employment. Difficulties of being on "home hours," like nights and weekends, and successfully juggling children's needs and work responsibilities, was reported by several of the mothers who worked outside of the home. Women discussed the challenge of managing the demands of a 24/7 work schedule while trying to balance bath time, homework, recitals, ball games, afterschool activities, and bedtime routines.

Although having workplace hours that never officially turn off seems to affect both genders, managing home responsibilities at the same time as dealing with work requirements appears to place more taxing demands on the female. And now, especially in the era where technology is everywhere, it seems nearly impossible to turn off the 24/7 work culture.

The lack of support systems was another challenge women identified when trying to manage family responsibilities and a demanding career. Unlike some men who have stay-at-home wives, the majority of women who have reached the upper echelons of their careers may not have the same level of support. Women tend to balance executive leadership roles at work and home responsibilities more often than their male counterparts.

One woman talked of the disparity and difficulty of juggling both, saying, "I had two kids and one of them was born with a heart condition right at the same time I was ready to take a big leap. And I said no, I'm going to wait. I think as a female you probably have that more so than you know. It's probably a sexist statement, but men just kind of go on."

Another participant said, "It's inevitable. One or the other always suffers. Generally when my career is going great, my mothering skills aren't doing well. When I feel I'm being a great mom, my work is usually not doing as well. Sometimes it changes day to day and other times it changes weekly or monthly. I rarely feel both are fantastic at the same time. I highly doubt men feel that way."

Another participant, a mother with two of her three children requiring special medical attention, discussed her dilemma, saying, "Do I really want to be home all day every day, or three days a week? That's a constant struggle for me. I don't have the magic answer. I know in my heart that I want to be there for my kids because in the blink of an eye they'll be grown. And I think even after the elementary stage, they'll be a lot more independent, where they won't need me as much. And I can work more, because I love working. I love what I do and my husband and I don't have any goals for me to stop working any time soon. So we just keep going where we are… because right now I have a six-month-old."

Only 9 percent of dual-earning marriages reported evenly sharing childcare, household tasks, and income earnings.

Although statistics don't currently exist yet, interviews with female and male executives demonstrate that males are beginning to take more supportive roles in the homes for their female executive spouses (Walsh, 2001). However, differences still exist, as typically the balance of home responsibilities is not evenly split. In fact, only 9 percent of dual-earning marriages reported they evenly shared childcare, household tasks, and income earnings (Milkie, Raley, & Bianchi, 2009).

Word on the Street

All too often, it's believed the reason most women quit their jobs after having kids is because they want to stay home with their children. Maybe these women *choose* to be home because they don't like to work as much as men do; they'd rather focus their efforts on home. Perhaps, overall, women aren't as ambitious as men. Do we even have the desire, the drive, to succeed as much as men do?

Emphatically, I argue yes! We're as ambitious as men and want to do as well, if not better, than our male colleagues. After all, why on earth would we go through the hoops of going to graduate school at such high numbers if we didn't have lofty aspirations? It's not that moms desire not to work, necessarily. Most often women feel stuck—in the middle of bosses who won't give an inch at work and husbands who won't carry their load at home.

As reported in *Getting to 50/50*, according to Joan Williams, director of work/life law at UC Hastings law school, "the truth is women leave reluctantly, after long, drawn-out efforts to find a way to stay, begging for small amounts of flexibility—which they are often refused" (Meers & Strober, 2009). In 2014 the Kaiser Family Foundation, in partnership with the *New York Times* and CBS News, conducted a survey of non-employed American adults between the ages of 25-54, with homemakers comprising about a quarter of their population.

Although a weak economy was cited as a cause of elimination of many jobs, women also reported the absence of family-friendly policies as a contributor to their lack of employment. According to the study, 61 percent of women indicated family duties were the reason they were not employed, in comparison to 37 percent of men. Nearly three-quarters of the women homemakers who hadn't searched for employment in the past year said they'd consider a job if it offered flexible hours, or an ability to work from home (Hamel, Firth, & Brodie, 2014).

Life at Home

All the participants who'd obtained C-level positions in healthcare spoke of how they wouldn't have been able to advance through the ranks of the corporate ladder had they not had family support. The majority of women who did have family help talked mainly of how supportive their spouses have been, although a few referred to having supportive work environments.

I can personally attest to the importance of spousal and family support in my own entrepreneurial journey and growing my company. My husband and I are equal partners, and that's the only way I've been able to manage having a growing business, get my doctoral degree, and raise a family at the same time. Of the women I talked to, 20 percent of the formal research participants spoke of switching caregiver roles with their husbands as a result of their advancing careers and increased earning potential.

One female said, "You really need to have a spouse who can be so flexible and so available. Which I have. I have been fortunate. We switched caregiver roles ten years ago when I came back and I started going through the ladder with the Catholic health system. He and I had the deliberate conversation, and we said, okay, obviously I have the much higher earning potential than he does, we need to switch care-giver roles. And that was really hard for me to do. I love be-ing a caregiver… For a female to advance, it's not impossible, but you've got to be such an equal partnership, but it takes a unique partner."

Although having a husband stay home with the family was not an alternative for the majority of women, some of them discussed the support systems they created with other work-ing moms, community resources, friends, neighbors, family members, or even hired assistance to ease some of the pres-sures. Even though those were viable solutions and had alle-viated some of the burden of responsibility for the mothers, many of them spoke of the guilt they felt having outsourced a portion of their home responsibilities.

One of the participants, Tammy, spoke of the internal conflict she battled regarding the need to have help with her daughter and the guilt she felt that she could not, in her mind, successfully juggle all the responsibilities of family and work. She acknowledged she needed to hire someone to help her, but she felt a sense of failure for not being able to handle it all with her rigorous work travel schedule, confiding, "I really struggle because my daughter is three and she's so strong-willed; she's actually just like me. I love her so much, but with traveling I feel like I'm missing a lot too. But I have worked so hard in my career to get ahead. I don't know how to balance being a good mom and a standout employee. I know I could alleviate some of the pressure I put on myself by hiring someone to help out around the house, but I feel like that's weakness—like I'm ad-mitting it's too much for me. I'm torn."

What Can Be Done: Succeeding as a Professional Mother at Home

It's unfortunate, and unrealistic, but professional mothers feel internal and external expectations to balance work and family on their shoulders, most of the time with minimal help—and do it all with perfection. Do you remember the old perfume commercial from the 1980s about how women can bring home the bacon and fry it up in a pan while never forgetting that she's your woman?

That theme continues to be pervasive in today's culture, and it's a dangerous message. The belief that professional working mothers are somehow flawed if they can't singlehandedly balance all the demands of the corporate boardroom, the kids' classrooms, and at the same time be a sexy wife, is damaging to a vast number of women who are internalizing that message and feeling as if they are failing.

I mean, seriously—when my kids' schools started allowing only store-bought items to be brought in for parties, as opposed to homemade goods, I was ecstatic. I was relieved that someone finally had the sense to cut some slack for working moms (albeit inadvertently, as they were more concerned with cooking hygiene) so they didn't have to bring home the bacon, *and* proceed to cook it, while wearing stilettos so he still knew he was your man, *and* bake cookies for the kids' party the next day, and do it all in the same damn night. And now with Pinterest detailing for you exactly how showroom perfect your house has to be…really? Do working people really live like that? And if they do, they can't have kids! It's ridiculous; something has to give.

The idea that women can grow their professional careers while also making their family life their number one priority is a reflection of conflicting notions of being the perfect mother—a balance of being completely devoted to children while enjoying a personally fulfilling career. For one, working mothers are often chastised for not making their family their main priority, as if working is considered being neglectful of their children.

However, studies show the opposite is true—women who

satisfy personal desires by working are more psychological-ly equipped for parenting (Dillaway & Pare, 2008). These dueling roles of balancing an advancing professional career with the fear of potentially neglecting your children results in women believing they must aspire to be a superwoman; this unattainable status can, and often does, lead women down the dangerous path of striving for perfection, where they expect to accomplish everything with the appearance of ease.

However, contrary to popular public opinion, or even just the "word on the street," women *can* have both—a fulfilling, successful career *and* family. In fact, research has conclud-ed that marriages, parents, and children can all thrive when both Mom and Dad have satisfying careers (Meers & Strober, 2009). When couples split the childcare duties and financial responsibilities, children are more fulfilled, moms experience less guilt, and dads are more connected to the family.

Study after study has concluded that the factors influencing a child's development two or three times more than daycare are when moms don't over-parent, dads are positively phys-ically and emotionally invested in their children's lives, and when the marriage is a healthy example of an emotionally connected relationship (Meers & Strober, 2009).

Being cared for exclusively by the mother is not positive-ly or negatively correlated to outcomes for children; as a re-sult, there's no data to prove, or reason to believe, children are harmed when the mother works outside the home. Therefore, societal pressures to stay home to do what's in the "best in-terests of the kids" are not based on facts, but opinions and emotions.

*Societal pressures to stay home to do
what's in the "best interest of the kids" are not
based on facts, but opinions and emotions.*

Careers help us determine our personal identities, sense of accomplishment, and fulfillment. Motherhood fulfills our internal desire to care for, nurture, and connect with another human on a soul level. Personally, I explain it as watching your heart walk around outside of yourself—there's no other relationship like it. However, being a mother can lead to the internal conflict between the roles of being a caretaker for our children at the same time as being a professional woman committed to advancing her career. So what's the solution?

First, let go of the guilt. It's not benefitting you or your family. In fact, research shows when a mother works she's teaching her kids about responsibility, so focus on that. Consider your perspective on how you tell your children you're going to work as well. I believe when a mom says, "I get to go to work today" it has a different impact on the children than "I have to go to work."

Also, unless you're a single parent, you're only half the parental equation in the home. Granted, some families have schedules that aren't conducive to both parents being home at the same time (travel, working nights/weekends, etc.), and that's completely understandable. But for those of you who do have both parents at home, I encourage you to get all hands on deck—and no time like the present to do it.

CHAPTER 3

Getting Your Spouse on Board

Marriage is not just spiritual communion and passionate embraces; marriage is also three meals a day, sharing the workload and remembering to carry out the trash.

~ JOYCE BROTHERS

As we've discussed, women reportedly opt out of their own careers for two reasons; the first being the weight of family responsibilities being too burdensome to manage on their own, and the second being because full-time work requirements are deemed not conducive to raising a family. We'll review both, but first let's discuss the home front. I don't know how active your spouse is around the house, but you have the potential to have a powerful ally in your corner.

Although it may take some getting used to, you'll probably need to relinquish some of the control you have when it comes to household responsibilities—just because it's not done the way you want it doesn't mean it's wrong. All too often we think our way is the only way things should be done, that we're right and everyone else is wrong. When we think this way it affects our actions and how receptive we are to any help offered. What affects the situation more than anything else happens to be your attitude.

And don't automatically think that just because your spouse

is male that he's unable, unwilling, or even just plain incompetent. I made that mistake while I was still in the hospital when my first daughter, Grace, was born. I was in the shower and heard her little newborn cry in the hospital room.

I hustled to get showered quickly, thinking my poor husband was sitting with a crying baby and had no clue what to do. I knew I'd just fed her so the next alternative was to change her diaper. Once out of the shower I went back into the hospital room and found my completely capable husband mid-diaper change. It was a joyous day because I knew I had a real partner in life and not some adult I had to add to my list of dependents.

When women start arguments at home, 80 percent of the time the fight is about the division of household chores (Coontz, 2006). It may seem too business-like and not "sexy" enough, but consider your marriage a working partnership.

How do you make a work project at the office successful? You talk. You plan. That's how home will be successful too. You create a game plan of who's going to do what (and when) in and around the house and you stick to it. If you need to veer off the plan or have additional one-time requests, then ask for a timeframe the project or task can be done in.

Remember, your emergency doesn't automatically become someone else's emergency. Also, gravitate toward tasks you enjoy doing (or at least don't hate) and that are fulfilling for you. You can even make a game of it—list off the tasks that need to be completed around the house and take turns picking the tasks for which you want to be responsible. For instance, I love to cook, but I loathe laundry. My husband stays on top of the clothes and I cook. I enlisted my kids' help for menu planning and each of us has a day of the week we get to decide what's for dinner.

You could find out your spouse's most despised chore and volunteer to do that one for him/her; it's better than getting a love letter! For instance, I hate getting gas in the car (all I can think about is how dirty those nasty, grimy handles are), but when I get in and see that my husband has filled up my tank, I get as giddy as a schoolgirl with a crush.

On the other hand, he loves it when the bed is made. I really couldn't care less if it is, but I know it matters to him. So I make a game out of it and try to make the bed as quickly as I can while he's getting ready for work. That's his love letter. Remember, you chose each other; you're on the same team.

As far as children go, the moment you let go of the concept that your offspring are solely your responsibility, the happier you'll be. When you both see your places as parents equally valuable, you're ensuring your children have two strong, healthy role models with whom to build solid relationships. Besides, kids benefit in incredible ways from having active, engaged dads in their lives; and dads benefit tremendously as well.

When Dad's Involved

When you make your spouse your ally, your true partner at home and in raising your children, you'll never be alone in facing the challenges of balancing work and home life. For your children, there's nothing like having a daddy active and involved in their life, and no amount of time spent with Mom can replace the relationship with him. The time they need from their father is a gift. It's unique; it's invaluable. And dads need their children, too, as they are great teachers of patience and perspective.

But for you and your spouse, the benefits are numerous too. Evidently, in American couples, when husbands complete 50 percent of the housework and wives contribute 50 percent of the earnings, the odds of divorce are reduced by 50 percent in comparison to households where the wife is responsible for all the home chores and the husband earns all the income

(Cooke, 2006; Meers & Strober, 2009).

Research even shows that working women have a greater sense of well-being than their non-working peers (whether they're moms or not), and women who obtain higher positions report the most fulfillment of them all (Barnett & Hyde, 2001). While we're talking about Dad and fulfillment for a minute, let's consider some ways Mom's job helps out, and not only to the family's bottom line. A 2016 study reported that as men took on more pressure and stress to carry the household financial responsibility, their physical health and psychological well-being were both negatively affected—with men's health being most affected during the years of being the sole breadwinner (MacMillan, 2016).

Overall, the level of resentment for your spouse and your children is also decreased by knowing you have someone else on your team to "do life" with. I know I'm a much better mom because I have a supportive husband—I have a stronger, deeper appreciation for my entire family when I'm around them.

When husbands complete 50 percent of the housework and wives contribute 50 percent of the earnings, the odds of divorce are reduced by 50 percent.

For you to continue in your role at work is just as important as it is for your spouse to participate in your family. Your husband will benefit more from you working than just having another paycheck. As evidenced, he actually has an opportunity for a more fulfilling career, a partner in marriage who's more than a roommate, and the gift of being able to have time to spend with your children.

Getting a Game Plan

Having help around the house will result in more equality between partners, shows children that household tasks are not gender-specific, reduces resentments, and supports happier relationships. When husbands engage in more household chores, wives experience less depression, marital discord decreases, and satisfaction increases (Coltrane, 2000).

As far as schedules and routines go, do what you can to make mornings, mealtimes, and bedtimes easier for everyone involved. Mornings may be easier if lunches are packed the night before, the following day's clothes are laid out, or when everyone bathes or showers in the evenings. Mealtimes have become quite a bit easier, at least in my house, with the pre-packaged meals that get delivered straight to the front door. If that's not an option, I know several people who spend Sundays prepping and cooking for the week so dinner is much less of struggle throughout the weekdays.

If your kids are old enough, I encourage you to get them involved with the chopping and measuring. Cooking together can be a great bonding time for you and your children or spouse. Or, another possibility for mealtimes is getting a Crock-Pot. Those things are fantastic! Plus, there are countless recipes online if you just look—and, bonus, the house always smells amazing when you get home.

When it comes to evenings and bedtimes, I live in the South and may not garner much support on this one, but I suggest a limit on the afterschool activities kids are involved in. I hear of children participating in every single sport in season, and I'm just not a proponent of that. Kids need time to play and be kids, as well as get adequate sleep. I have a two-sport maximum at a time for my kids, and that helps limit all of the shuffling and juggling of schedules. If your kids are involved in sports, you may want to consider carpooling with some of the other players. That has helped us out tremendously during seasons when my youngest daughter is involved in sports.

"Doing it all" doesn't have to mean all by yourself. Strong personal and professional support systems are needed to help alleviate some of the burden of responsibility on women, when attempting to balance motherhood with the demands of their careers. In fact, all of the participants with children in the formal study acknowledged they were only able to move up in their careers as a result of support they received with rearing their children. Even the participants who spoke of having additional support stated their family responsibilities were still considered one of the challenges they had to balance; however, they credited the help they received at home as what allowed them to successfully move up the corporate ladder.

Support doesn't always equate to having someone help care for the children either. Support can be provided in a variety of ways; be creative with what works for you and your family's needs, budget, and the likely self-deprecating internal monologue running rampant in your head. Perhaps you need to outsource the housekeeping, grocery shopping, laundry, or personal appointment setting for the family.

For our family, I was able to find help through an online source devoted to connecting caregivers with families. If you don't need someone full-time then you possibly may even be able to split the responsibility and pay with a friend or another family in your neighborhood. There really are countless ways to access help in balancing household duties—if you allow yourself to get past the guilt.

Even if you don't outsource home chores, you can still enlist the help of the family troops. Believe me, if kids are skilled enough to work a smart device, then they're definitely skilled enough to wash some dishes or fold some clothes. And, above all, you're teaching them responsibility.

There are a number of options to explore and resources available. I encourage you to find a good fit for your family, someone trustworthy and reliable, to help you balance the responsibilities of home life with the demands of your career.

With this perspective, career-driven females often feel rejuvenated and a new sense of being able to "have it all" and successfully balance what they have.

Despite traditional American beliefs, research has evidenced that children benefit tremendously when they see both Mom and Dad work—they grow socially, cognitively, and excel in their independence and self-confidence. Because of the balance of responsibilities, children of working moms also benefit from having strong relationships with both parents. Not to mention the fact that when Mom has an income, the immense pressure and stress of the family's financial security is not all on Dad's shoulders. Two paychecks provide a margin of protection and security.

There are clearly going to be obstacles when both parents work, but the advantages far exceed the challenges. As reported by Meers and Strober, according to Janice Steil, psychology professor at Adelphi University, "husbands and wives are more satisfied with their relationships when women and men regard themselves as equally responsible for providing financially for the family, as compared to those who see the husband as responsible for providing. These couples had a greater likelihood of confiding and showing affection, and the wives were less likely to be depressed" (Meers & Strober, 2009, p. 52).

In fact, countless studies have examined the link between women, work, and depression; working women have a lower risk of depression than those who are not employed (Barnett & Hyde, 2001). Women who climb higher up the ladder report the most fulfillment of all. So now that you're aware of the benefits of staying in your job—and moving up if you want— let's consider some ways to make that possible.

We've already talked about how women do want to succeed as much, if not more so, than men in the workplace. However, we often fall into the mind-set dictated by history—telling ourselves that "it's going to be hard, if not impossible, so why even try?" Consider this, though: anything worth doing is going to be a challenge. If it were easy, everyone would do it.

CHAPTER 4

Dust Off Your Courage

Yes, I have doubted. I have wandered off the path, but I always return. It is intuitive, an intrinsic, built-in sense of direction. I seem always to find my way home.

~ HELEN HAYES

Women, it's time we begin to speak candidly about what we want in the workplace. Not in a brazen, confrontational way. But if we want to succeed, then we need to make a bigger effort to communicate our needs. For example, men are more apt to apply for positions and promotions when they have about 60 percent of the qualifications; women, on the other hand, wait until they have every qualification required before they feel comfortable holding their hand up and saying they are capable.

As a result, women internalize the message by telling themselves they've been passed over, when all they really needed to say was, "Hey—I'm qualified and competent. I want to be considered for the position!"

Stuffing our problems in silence does nothing to get to a resolution; the only way to resolve an issue is by communicating in a respectful, brave way—to the person who can do something about the issue, not to your friends around the water cooler. Don't hesitate to take a stand for yourself; life is too short to suffer in silence, with growing resentment and anger. Besides, oftentimes when you get angry you misuse your own energy, leading to ineffective results. You can't control what's said or done, but you can control how you receive and react to the message.

Be secure in voicing your concerns; that security comes from being crystal clear in knowing what you want and having a game plan on how you're going to achieve it. Stand your ground without pointing fingers and remove your emotions from the situation.

Take, for example, my friend Kate, who is a brilliant, highly-qualified saleswoman who was affected by the economic downturn in 2008, being laid off from a great position. As a result of personal circumstances, she found herself in a role where she'd been hired for outside sales, but her manager would only allow her to cold call from the office, as she didn't want her leaving the building (which completely defeats the purpose of being an outside salesperson). Kate knew she'd never be successful in a cold call position.

She and I discussed her options and made a game plan. She arranged a meeting with her supervisor and presented the alternatives: Kate proposed that she be given two months to get out of the office and make sales calls, and show the company she could be successful in the role she was hired for. As she explained to her boss, if she wasn't successful, she would happily come back in the office and continue to cold call. Kate was able to prove her worth and value to the company by removing her emotion, presenting the facts, and creatively standing up for herself, as opposed to letting her feelings get the best of her.

Which brings us to another issue: sometimes creative work arrangements are required to help working mothers stay in the game. Many women think work is black and white, that it's all or nothing. However, as you'll see, that's not necessarily the case. Work can have a lot of flexibility—if you earn it.

Part-Time Work: Real-Time Talk

First, the good news: some workplace policies benefit working moms, and when employers allow for creative supports (like reporting to the office early or having on-site daycare) the number of women in management is raised (Meers & Strober, 2009). That's great news, actually, because we'll never get to equality without more women in management.

There are multitudes of ways to keep your irons in the fire, but they most likely require you to be creative—and flexible. As a working mom, instead of asking yourself how you're going to manage it all, consider asking yourself how you're going to keep your skills sharp. First, make it a point to find a company culture that's conducive to supporting employees and their families. If you're not in one now, find one. Remember, you and your skills are valuable commodities. When you're on the job search, research the company; interview them as much as they're interviewing you.

But now for some frank talk. If you go part-time, you'll take a financial hit for reducing your hours. Be prepared. It's fair. It's worth it. Also be prepared, however, to have a full-time commitment. Don't go in with a "clock in, clock out, and run like hell when it's time to go" or an "I'm just part-time" attitude. There may be times when you're needed to work longer and harder on certain projects or deadlines that come up. Again, that's fair. It's worth it.

When you're working on reduced hours (or even if you aren't), commit to ensuring you and your team are working as efficiently as possible. Determine each day how you can add the most value to the organization in the most effective way. Gone are the days of long, unproductive meetings where you leave and question if anything got accomplished. Go to meetings with your goals determined, and ask the other attendees to define and relay their goals too. If possible, schedule short meetings—30 minutes at a maximum—and require clarity and direction while moving toward conclusions.

Keep Going

I'm sure all of us, at some point in our careers, have been dealt a bad hand at work. I know I have and so have the women I interviewed. When that happens, take a deep breath and consider your options—long term. Don't be quick to throw in the towel. The best question to ask yourself is, "How can I make a difference?" not "Can I quit?" You may need to change the rules where you work, change your work environment, or even go out on your own, but don't quit pursuing your career.

You can be committed to both your family and your work by remembering that you're in charge. You determine where to focus your time and efforts, both at work and at home. If your desires to try a different path are met with, "Well, we've always done it this way," then have a bold, brave attitude with a fighting spirit and say, "Great! There's a first time for everything. How can we do it differently?" There'll be skeptics who think you can't balance it all. Keep showing up; prove them wrong!

Above all else, however, release those unrealistic expectations of yourself that drive you to perfectionism. It's crazy to think you must attend every single child's practice, game, or event. Share that responsibility with your spouse and pick the events you can make. Keep your expectations of yourself in check at work as well. Don't feel obligated to work yourself to death.

I have a friend who's the primary breadwinner for her family and she'd made it her life to work nonstop. Finally, after several blowups from her family, she put her foot down. She realized she has to have boundaries in all areas of life. Now, if she has a meeting after hours, then her office knows she'll attend virtually. It's what she needed to do to balance both worlds.

In all actuality, your nemesis is probably not your peers, your boss, your clients, or your nonstop meetings. It's probably fear, which is fed by the still, small voice in your head telling you you can't do it all. You look around and see other people successfully blending work and family but you feel you can't. Well, yes—you can. It's work, but it's also having the belief and attitude of staying open to whatever it takes to make this happen. You're in a season of life, but this, too, shall pass. Don't check out. Keep your eye focused on the goal. You've got this!

For Leaders at Work

Americans, both male and female, have been fooled into the false belief that more is better, especially when it comes to work. In our global economy, organizations are wrought with managers who believe working 24/7 is the only way to succeed, priding themselves on how many hours they put in at the office. Burning the midnight oil sends a message that you're tough, committed, and irreplaceable. However, that perspective doesn't take efficiency, productivity, or innovation into consideration—which should all be the focus instead.

When companies need to widen their scope, typically the first response is to throw more hours and warm bodies at the problem. We get busy, tied up in the tornado of work, without stepping back to see how we can work more efficiently with current time and resources. Those who work the longest hours aren't necessarily a company's biggest contributors, though. Employee incentives should focus more on creatively finding more ways to be effective and efficient at work. Be committed to taking the fat out of your workday.

The only surety in the world is that change is constant—and the current work environment is no exception. As a result, those employees who successfully mold and adapt to changing priorities are truly valuable assets. The ability to quickly adjust to organizational shifts is not only beneficial, it's necessary. The same goes for employees and their needs; organizations must begin to be more flexible with their demands on employees.

In the current world of constant connectivity, it would seem that flexible options such as working from home, delaying work start time, or ending the day a little later for some employees should be commonplace. However, it's astounding how few companies offer a variety of flexible options to most of the employees—an estimated 20 percent (Bernard, 2014). A reported 38 percent of companies offer some of their employees the ability to work from home on a consistent basis (Families and Work Institute, 2014). In fact, much of the existing research states companies are flexible because they self-report that they are; but the truth is not the reality of the situation. What can be done?

Flexible workplace arrangements are not all-or-nothing solutions. Providing flexibility for employees can come in a variety of forms, considering what's most suitable for the company's needs. Some creative options are having company "quiet time" where interruptions aren't allowed two to three mornings a week. More can be done in less time if we allow fewer interruptions and help each other more.

Also, flexible choices include such arrangements as semi-flexible work hours, staggered shifts, or allowing employees to occasionally work from home. Companies can also have family-friendly programs or policies set in place to protect employees so they aren't penalized for having altered schedules. But the key to this type of program's effectiveness is making the policy as transparent as possible, not leaving enforcement to the discretion of individual managers.

Allowing flexible scheduling options for employees makes

it sound like the company's doing the employee a favor, right? Flexible workplace arrangements also benefit the employer. First, the company gains improved employee retention. In turn, improved retention lowers turnover and creates happier, more engaged, committed employees. Decreased turnover also results in less time and money spent on new hire trainings.

Another result of offering more flexibility in the workplace is the benefit of a wider talent pool, as a more flexible environment opens up options for new sources of talent. When companies provide options other than eight-to-five office jobs, talented candidates traditionally unavailable to work within those parameters now become potential employees.

Overall: be the boss, or employer, you'd want to work for. If you're a manager, I encourage you to not evaluate your employees based on the number of hours they put in but on what they do with the time they're there. Although time is a valuable commodity, it should not be the sole currency in which someone's commitment to his or her job is determined.

Change the corporate culture from one that values time put in at your desk to one that values the talent each employee adds to the team. Have specific, obtainable productivity standards for each role. And, reward your top producers with the leverage and flexibility to work differently. Be the boss who accommodates employees when their performance has earned it.

When working moms have the skills and experience that fit the needs of the organization, but they need more flexibility in their schedules, do whatever's possible to accommodate them. Be creative with scheduling, even if the schedule adjustments are for part of the time. Make adjustments that are in the best interests of both parties to ensure your company retains its talent, or it's likely you'll be looking for their replacements.

Wrapping Up

The challenge of raising a family while advancing a professional career was identified as the first obstacle women reported experiencing. Every woman interviewed, both formally and informally, discussed the difficulty of trying to have some semblance of family life balanced with the demands and needs of a professional life. Support systems and help with family responsibilities were key to women advancing their careers through the ranks of employment.

Another integral piece of the puzzle would be solved if more social support were given to working mothers. As a society, we've embraced the faulty notion that children are somehow harmed when they're reared in families where the mother enjoys a full-time career; in fact, the opposite is true. Research has evidenced that employed women benefit from improved financial security, greater stability in marriage, better health, and even report living a more fulfilled life. It's time we have more representation of happy mothers with high-achieving careers, as that's a better depiction of reality than what's currently presented in media.

I want it to be clear that I'm not judging other women for choosing a different path than I've chosen for my family and me. That's far from the truth. I support that we all have choices and have to do what we feel is in the best interests for our children. I know how quickly they grow up, as my oldest has now graduated from college and lives out of state. However, if we, as females, want to ever achieve equality in the organizational ranks, then we have to do more to support the employed mothers in the workforce. Without a doubt, children need their parents to attend to, love, nurture, and care for them. And just because a mother is employed outside the home doesn't mean she's incapable of providing her children with a secure, loving home.

The desire for support in the professional setting most often talked about was the need for more flexible scheduling. I hypothesize that if employers offered more creative solutions to scheduling for employees with family responsibilities, both male and female, more mid-level high potential women would be willing and available to fill the gender gaps in the boardrooms. Working nonstop no longer assures us security in our positions at work, the promotion we were counting on, or the raise we wanted. However, it does guarantee a family that doesn't see their dad much. As a society, we need leadership to include moms who are completely involved at work and dads who are completely engaged at home too.

Now, let's move along to the second challenge professional women face.

PART TWO
Where We Stand

It wasn't a shocking revelation that women discussed the difficulties of balancing family needs, household responsibilities, and an advancing career. In fact, if those with children hadn't mentioned it, I'd think something was wrong! However, the remaining three obstacles women talked about came as a bit of a shock to me. I presume the idea that we're terminally unique happens to everyone. You know, that idea that everyone else has it all together and no one else on earth could possibly understand, relate to, or be going through exactly what you are.

Well, good news: you're not alone. Every woman I talked to experienced challenges in her journey, in one form or another. The remaining three obstacles are presented, along with strategies and advice to overcome them when they occur in your life. But first, let's discuss the second challenge women are dealing with in their career journeys.

Women found themselves in situations where they felt challenged in their careers, which was an obstacle first identified in my formal research study. However, several of the informal study participants employed in other industries expressed similar sentiments, but not all for the same reasons. The common causes identified in both groups were: being limited in advancement opportunities; limited by family challenges (as covered in the previous chapter); and limited by age.

CHAPTER 5

Where Can I Go from Here?

*I just love bossy women. I could be around
them all day. To me, bossy is not a pejorative term at all.
It means somebody's passionate and engaged and
ambitious and doesn't mind leading.*

~ AMY POEHLER

Of the 80 percent of women who identified feeling limited because of being challenged by present circumstances, about half discussed how they'd reached the highest position available within their current organizations. They discussed having desires to further their careers in healthcare, but advancing either required relocation or leaving their current employer.

In every case, they were extremely happy with their present employer and leadership team, and weren't actively looking to change companies. However, they desired to be more challenged in their roles. "I'm facing challenges now because I'm as high up as I can go in this organization," one participant relayed. "I love what I'm doing, but it's this conflict of what to do to keep my career advancing."

Another woman spoke of how people in her company were working until later in life, creating limited availability for open positions. She said, "Now, if I wanted to leave the organization then yes, the sky's the limit. But I don't really have any desire to do that." In many situations women relayed feeling torn between staying where they were and choosing to leave.

Our American society views professional ambition as an option for women but a requirement for men.

It's no surprise that leadership roles become fewer as you rise through the organizational ranks; however, is that a limitation that specifically affects women's rise to the top? I believe it is, especially if you consider the fact that we don't operate our work life in silos; meaning we're navigating through increasingly demanding organizational ranks where females are fewer in number, while also trying to balance all the other requirements personal/family life presents.

Which leads us to another point: women are less likely to strive to attain leadership roles than men. In fact, when I was on my dissertation journey and had chosen my committee, I presented them with my topic because I needed their blessing to continue. One committee member challenged me on that topic, prompting me to consider the alternative to my assumption that all women strive to hold positions of leadership, and that somehow external forces are keeping them down. He proposed the notion that perhaps women were not in executive roles because they chose not to be. Although I vehemently denied the possibility that women were holding themselves back, the research proved it to be true. How and what we can and should accomplish in life is in large part formed by societal expectations.

Bossy: The Other "B" Word

Oftentimes when girls make attempts to lead, they're labeled bossy, whereas boys are more apt to be recognized for taking initiative. When boys demonstrate assertive behaviors, society typically responds positively, supporting their efforts and calling them leaders; girls who take leadership into their own hands aren't met with such enthusiasm and excitement. Generally, their efforts to lead are thwarted with negativity, disdain, and even sabotage.

I'll never forget being at the end of my seventh grade school year and the list of students who made National Junior Honor Society (NJHS) was posted. I checked the list simply to see who else made it, because I didn't question my acceptance. I always made A-honor roll and was in gifted and talented courses, so I thought it was a given that I'd be accepted into NJHS.

Well, shockingly, my name was nowhere on the list. All my friends were accepted to the covetous group of soon-to-be-eighth-grade scholars, but I hadn't been included. My dad, who raised me, was furious, and called a meeting with all my teachers, the counselors, and the principals to find out what kept me from getting in.

After all the details were hashed out, it came down to the fact that my seventh grade history teacher hadn't voted for me because she felt I was too "bossy" and didn't work well with others. I used to take group projects and either assign the roles of what everyone was responsible for, or, most often, I'd just take the damn project and do it myself so I could ensure it was completed exactly how I wanted it done!

Instead of helping me use what was perhaps one of my greatest strengths, my teacher deemed it my biggest weakness and didn't support and encourage me to work more collaboratively with my peers. I could have been taught to work better with others in group settings by learning to see and value others' strengths. But instead I was punished for my early attempts at leadership. Would that have been the case if I'd been a male? We'll never know…

How does this transition into the working world of today?

Well, it's true that most positions of leadership are filled by men, leaving women with self-fulfilling prophecies that they shouldn't expect to attain positions of leadership—so they don't. And, quite possibly, women are living with the same patterns and beliefs they experienced and had reinforced for them through childhood.

Another bias that exists against women was confirmed in a 2012 research study when scientists reviewed identical resumes submitted from both genders for a student lab manager position. Although the resumes were the same, both male and female scientists deemed the female applicant less competent, offering her less mentoring and lower starting pay (Moss-Racusin et al., 2012).

Gender bias affects how performance is viewed, most often lowering our assessments of women but raising our evaluation of men. As a result, even when women feel confident enough to attempt to apply to positions of leadership, they're faced with blatant gender discrimination.

Family Issues

Some of my participants referred specifically to family limitations as the root of their current challenges. One participant, a mother of six, spoke about her desire to advance her career, but her family was content where they lived. She didn't know how to take advantage of other employment opportunities, as they'd require additional travel and/or relocation. As a result, she came to the difficult, personal decision to stay in her current role and decline the offers, putting her family desires ahead of her personal ones. As the sole income earner for the family, she decided to do what she felt was in the best interest of her family and stay in the region where she was currently employed.

Another woman, a mother of three, spoke of the challenges of raising two children with special healthcare needs. She said,

"I think men get their value from their work. Women, if they have a family, run the household more often than the men do. So when they have the household and the office to run, depending on the stressors at home, it can be too much. For me, some days are better than others. Some days I don't feel like I know how to balance at all."

CHAPTER 6

Time to Stay? Or Go?

Age to me means nothing. I can't get old; I'm working.
I was old when I was twenty-one and out of work.
As long as you're working, you stay young.

~ GEORGE BURNS

One obstacle I hadn't anticipated or considered prior to conducting the formal study was that 50 percent of the women were presently facing age-related obstacles. They spoke candidly about feeling they reached huge heights in their careers but knew their current and future advancement opportunities were limited because of their age.

Some of them explained how they were satisfied with their current positions but didn't know if they should be looking for a new career opportunity before getting what they felt was too old. One stated, "Do I think I see myself staying at [employer] through the remainder of my career? I don't think so because I'm fairly young. But I will say that it's a barrier that is coming to bear itself now, getting asked often about how many years I expect to work."

Another participant relayed, "I love what I'm doing, but at my age, which is fifty-four, I really should probably leave and do something else, go somewhere else before it's too late. It's probably not the smartest career decision to stay where I am, even though I love it. I love it here and it's been a blessing to come here every day. So it's like, 'Really? Do I really have to think about leaving?' But I'd say that's a regret. If you interviewed me ten years from now, I think I'd say I regretted staying in one place so long."

One woman spoke of the uneasiness of not knowing her next step. "For the first time in a long time, I don't know what I want to do next. I have no clue. I made this career change for a lot of reasons 18 months ago and I don't know for how long. I don't know if I want to retire here. I have no idea what my next step is." She wasn't alone in this dilemma. Many women echoed feeling they were at a crossroads and were unsure how to proceed.

Here's the Good News

It's apparent that challenges are inevitable in life and careers. Women will face a variety of obstacles in all industries, positions, levels of responsibilities, and at all ages. Besides, isn't that all life is—a series of challenges and obstacles, with great experiences as a result? The struggle identified was that many women currently feel challenged in their roles because of lack of advancement opportunities, family responsibilities, and age.

No matter what career stage a woman finds herself in, challenges will be part of the journey. There are several ways to navigate through the labyrinth if you're experiencing career obstacles right now. However, it depends on the reason for your struggle. The following are suggestions the employee and the employer can do to deal with the difficulties of limited advancement and then the challenge of age.

If you're currently employed, it's both yours and your employer's responsibility to help you navigate career challenges in order to be successful, motivated, and loyal. Depending on the level of your role, you can talk to your supervisor or the human resources department about advancement opportunities; or, you might need to reach out to a corporate recruiter to discuss your options outside of your current employer.

I can tell you from personal experience, I've dealt with the obstacle of being currently challenged. It's scary. Although I'm the owner and CEO of my own healthcare organization, I worked myself out of a job before I'd reached my fortieth birthday. Reinventing myself or trying to figure out my next steps was not an easy task. Some days I felt I was doing a great job and making phenomenal progress. Other days I felt I was navigating through an obstacle course blind-folded in heels. It's a very real fear and it can happen to both genders, at any age.

Thankfully, I was in a situation where I had the chance to pursue a personal goal I'd had since becoming a single, teenage mom. I was finally in a position where I had the time and ability to return to school and obtain my doctorate degree. But that's when I felt the real challenge begin. I was at a place where I was done with school and didn't really have any day-to-day responsibilities at work. I had to determine what I could possibly do next by asking myself what would fulfill me personally and professionally.

That has led me on another quest; I've been focusing my time and attention on starting and growing a new business venture. It's been fun and exciting, but it's also hard and trying at times. I enjoy building businesses, so I'm grateful to be in a position to follow my passion and watch it flourish.

If you're in that place of uncertainty right now, I recommend finding an executive coach or career coach to help you navigate the muddy waters. It's easy to be too close to your own situation. It's that whole "can't see the forest for the trees" concept. It's hard to see something right in front of you. An effective coach will provide you with personalized, unbiased, straightforward assistance to gain perspective and navigate your options.

In the event you choose to leave your current organization, a career coach will also give you feedback on your resume and practice interviewing with you. You'll be provided with dedicated time to improving your skills, as well as being held accountable for your progress.

If you don't have the financial resources available for a coach, talk to colleagues, relatives, or friends about your strengths, weaknesses, interests, and desires. Ask them to be upfront and honest with you, but be ready to put aside your defenses (they get you nowhere anyway). Conduct an online search for careers that capitalize on the strengths you've identified. When you find two to three good matches, do more research on companies that offer those positions. The world is open to you; you just have to be open to exploring other options.

While we're on the subject of exploring other options and possibly being out of your comfort zone, I'd also encourage you to broaden your network of colleagues, peers, mentors, and advisors. Networking is crucial, and appears to be one area women aren't as comfortable as men. When men are out on the golf course they aren't just playing—they're building relationships and expanding their networks.

Pocket Opportunities List: Your Personal Board of Directors

One thing I had to do when I was in school was create a list of my top five to ten contacts who were my "Pocket Opportunities." It was a list of people (names, emails, phone numbers, etc.) I knew and admired, who I was able to turn to for career advice and mentorship when I was in my season of challenge.

I encourage you to create your own pocket opportunities

list of people you know. Consider this list to be your personal board of directors, people you can go to at a moment's notice for advice, a reference, a referral, or even a job if you need one. Ensure your list is made of people with whom you have a direct relationship, even if it's been minimal contact in the past. It's an invaluable tool and can come in handy when you're in time of need.

Try to reach out quarterly (at a minimum) to the people on your list, even if you don't have anything pressing to talk about. Check in with them, or even ask them if they need anything from you. Tell them you value their feedback and input. Then, when you do need them they'll be more apt to help you in your circumstance, because you've made it a point to maintain a personal relationship. You never know how a relationship will evolve when you're invested in your own growth, and the growth of someone you know and care about.

For instance, I met Lauren a few years ago when she was working at a retail store near my house. I'd gone into the store to order trunks for my daughters' trip to summer camp and Lauren was the friendliest, most helpful sales associate I'd ever met. When I told her what camp the girls went to, she was thrilled, as she had grown up attending that camp and had also been a counselor there for a few summers. Lauren was so genuine and friendly that we exchanged numbers and she quickly became our go-to babysitter.

Fast-forward several years and an evolved relationship with Lauren and our family. Lauren is now in her senior year of college (studying for her dream job—to be an eighth-grade history teacher) and we still have contact with her. She has started her own jewelry business while in college and is doing phenomenally well.

Over the past Christmas break, she reached out and asked me to mentor her. She provided me the parameters of what her request entailed, which was to go to dinner once a month when she was home, so we can discuss her career goals, plans, and what she's doing to accomplish them.

I was honored to be asked, but also proud of her for being proactive and taking the initiative to chart her own course. After all, navigating her career path is in her hands and she's not leaving it up to whim or chance. We meet and discuss what's going on in my life, too, but my true focus is to help her watch out for blind spots, especially with her new business venture. Her enthusiasm for life is contagious and she's a joy to be around.

Although this is an example of a personal mentor-mentee relationship, it can serve to be how a business mentor relationship can evolve. We will talk more about mentorship later, but know your future is in your hands and is too valuable to leave up to potentially missed opportunities.

CHAPTER 7

Creating Opportunities

*People will accomplish more if they are
given an opportunity to use their talents and
abilities in the way they work best.*

~ DAVID PACKARD

Feeling your advancement is limited at your workplace is a problem—for both employees and employers. When female employees have limited opportunities for advancement the employer risks losing high-potential, high-performing talent. Employers are encouraged to organize or support internal or external peer groups for these women.

These peer groups can be structured in a way that provides employees the ability to collaborate and share ideas for constructively dealing with their current challenges. An external or internal executive coach could facilitate the group to ensure it remains productive and on task (and doesn't become a gripe session).

Another opportunity to retain top talent, despite having limited or no advancement prospects currently available, is to provide women with mentor or team lead roles, paid or unpaid. At my company we were able to create lead roles for therapists and it has worked very well. The supervising management staff was thankful for having more clinical support, and the therapists who became leads have enjoyed the added responsibility. This supports employee engagement and increases feelings of purpose and value, despite the current lack of advancement opportunities.

From an employer perspective, creating a position or opportunity for high-potential employees makes sound business sense, in that you've planned for succession in the event a higher up position becomes available. From an employee perspective, having your company and/or boss create a role for you because you're such a valuable asset to their organization is the ultimate acknowledgement of your worth, making the arrangement a win-win.

Employer-supported volunteer work has also proven to create a sense of purpose, perspective, and camaraderie. For instance, my company has sponsored and supported employee-organized canned food, coat, and toy drives—just to name a few. It's been fun watching everyone's commitment and excitement to the cause grow, and they've made it extremely competitive too.

One year we chose to support a local food bank and participated in a food drive. The entire office was divided up by departments and the race to get the most food in the donation boxes began with a vengeance. When it was all over, food was abundant and the camaraderie and playful competition was contagious. Employee morale was high and the number of families who benefited was astonishing.

We also have a C.A.R.E. committee (C.A.R.E. stands for our company core values: Commitment, Accountability, Results, and Ethics) made up of volunteer employees who meet to discuss employee engagement initiatives and staff appreciation ideas. Prior to the formation of the C.A.R.E. committee, the company executive leadership team (myself included) would discuss and decide ways to engage and reward the employees. But, as you may know, people are motivated to do well for varying reasons.

The best solution, we concluded, was to empower the employees who wanted to be more engaged with the ability to do so. Researching ideas, presenting requests for approval, and creating budgets for projects has been empowering for them on a whole different level, compared to when the ideas came from the executive team.

The key is to creatively think of ways to engage employees in the workplace when advancement opportunities are limited. Even if there are no initiatives currently in place, ask your valued employees to help create them. This will ensure not only that those initiatives get done, but you'll also obtain easier employee buy-in, improved morale, and possibly added succession planning, which is crucial to the project's and company's success.

Women who reported feeling currently challenged because of their age spoke candidly of how committed they were to their work. They reported not knowing what to do to stay involved in their employment, since they felt they were at a juncture in life. Engaging in either formal mentoring programs, or possibly providing informal support to high-potential women within the company, are two options for finding more involvement within the organization.

If a formal mentorship program doesn't exist, don't let that stop you. Help create one. Also, volunteer work, non-profit support, or an external mentorship program (like Big Brothers Big Sisters) are great ways to diversify your life experiences apart from your employer.

American workers in the 21st century, both male and female, are employed well beyond what had previously been identified as retirement age. Organizations can capitalize on the wisdom and knowledge of these more senior workers prior to their retirement. Consider implementing a group or individual mentorship program to engage top-level leaders who can identify, support, and advise the company's pool of future leadership.

Another way senior employees can be more involved in employment efforts is to assist the company with recruiting initiatives. The employees can't only be involved with recruiting prospective talent, but once the new candidates are hired, the senior employee can be assigned to mentor them as well. The opportunities are endless, once you realize and tackle the real issue.

When you boil it down, the real issue is this: people have a basic need to feel valued and engaged at their place of employment, regardless of their age and position. They desire to feel their presence and commitment matters—as though something in the core of their being is fulfilled. Employees need to be motivated and engaged.

According to Alise Cortez, Ph.D., an employee engagement researcher, "employee engagement is about three things: challenge, creativity, and leadership, and the ability to take those three things to the next level. It's not a one-size-fits-all model. Great leaders and managers uniquely understand what activates each person by knowing what each person wants, then devising that path and development plan for them."

I often get asked why I started my own pediatric home health care agency, and the answer is always the same. I wasn't appreciated, valued, or engaged where I was. At the time I started my company, I worked for another agency and overheard the owners talking and laughing about how they believed all their employees were replaceable. I was appalled. I couldn't believe what I heard.

Rather than continue to work for people who didn't appreciate their employees, or go somewhere else and possibly be an undervalued worker again, I decided to open my own agency, with the sole intent to honor, appreciate, and respect my employees. There have definitely been some growing pains, but they've all been worth it when I have people come up to me and say their job at KidsCare Therapy is the best job they've ever had! That's been the most rewarding part of the entire journey.

The Bottom Line

There are several ways companies can provide engagement opportunities for employees who currently feel challenged. However, it depends on the reason for the struggle. No matter in which career stage you or your employees find yourself, challenges will be part of the journey. High-achieving professionals, both men and women, typically have achievement and advancement in their bones; it runs in their blood.

As a result, women identified being challenged in their roles because of limited advancement, family responsibilities, and their age. But the good news is there are ways to move past those challenges. I've given you a few suggestions to think about, but there are others, I'm sure. Consider what works for you and make it happen!

PART THREE

In a Bind

The issue of gender disparity and the pay differential for women in comparison to men seems to be all over the news recently; however, we can talk about it until we're blue in the face, but what's actually working to solve the problem? I started the research journey with a couple of assumptions in mind, but not many. My goal was to put aside any bias and learn as much new information as I could.

Every researcher should begin his or her journey with a commitment to eliminating as many preconceived ideas, beliefs, and experiences and let the data speak for itself—so that's what I tried to do. I was intrigued by the statistics of how many females climbed to mid-level management positions but how the upper-level executive roles were seemingly uninviting to females. I wanted to get to the bottom of what was keeping so many of us from reaching the top, as women in corporate America continue to deal with a huge gender gap for senior-level positions and pay.

According to a McKinsey & Company report (2015), based on the rate of progress made since 2012, it's estimated that it will take 25 years to obtain gender equality at the senior-VP level, and more than 100 years in the C-suite. Yeah, you read that right—100 years! So, basically not even our granddaughters will be able to experience workplace equality in their lifetime. Well, not on my watch! I was determined to find out what the other issues were, as determining the cause is half the battle.

All the women spoke of their own unique, personal obstacles they'd encountered and overcome on their career journeys. Regardless of the industry in which the interviewee was employed, clear themes surfaced from the conversations. I knew trying to balance family needs with a demanding workplace role was going to be high up on the list of challenges, so when that became apparent I was clearly not shocked.

I was, though, fairly surprised to find out such a high percentage of the women discussed dealing with current struggles as a result of limited advancement opportunities and navigating career decisions when considering their age. Initially I didn't think that was an obstacle specific to women. However, this challenge is complicated by the fact that there seems to be limited opportunities for positions open to women as they advanced into higher organizational ranks. But I wasn't prepared for what came next. The third obstacle really threw me for a loop, just not for reasons I'd anticipated.

Obstacle Three: Gender Is An Issue

Most of the women I talked to, whether in female-dominated industries or male-dominated ones, discussed gender bias and being female in the upper echelons as the third obstacle they encountered. Even though evidence supports that women are necessary, highly productive leaders capable of producing high-caliber results, we're still dealing with a noticeable absence of females in executive-level positions (McDonagh & Paris, 2013; McKinsey & Company, 2015).

In many workforce sectors, including healthcare, a large proportion of male executives are employed in top-level roles, and the majority of females are found in middle-management positions (Weil & Mattis, 2001). In all sectors, substantially more men than women have obtained positions in upper management. In fact, the proportionate amount of females in executive-level positions is greater in healthcare than in comparison to other settings.

Now, I know there's been specific controversy over the whole gender pay disparity issue and how the data has been calculated, but let's consider looking at just the details for healthcare, since that's the industry I researched and with which I'm the most familiar. Despite the fact that equal levels of education and experience were reported in 2011, women earned, on average, approximately $134,100 annually; for men, the figure was $166,900.

Therefore, women reportedly earned $32,800, or 20 percent, less per year than their male counterparts (American College of Healthcare Executives, 2012). Disparity? Yes, I do believe so. Even with all the recent attention the subject has received, it remains a problem. Let's look at a few reasons that contribute to the issue.

Sources of the Problem

Leadership: Damned If You Do; Doomed If You Don't

Workplace societal norms, which have traditionally been regarded as masculine, contribute to play a role in influencing women's careers (Babcock & Laschever, 2007; Catalyst, 2007). These male-dominated norms have affected women by resulting in barriers and an imbalance of power for them when attempting to move up the career ladder. We have to look more closely at this male-dominated authority if we're ever going to figure out how women have successfully climbed their way into executive positions and pay, and can continue to do so.

Over the years, several attempts have been made to attribute leadership characteristics to men and women; in fact, this has been an ongoing debate. Certain people think specific leadership traits and behaviors are tied to men, and believe women demonstrate different styles and characteristics of leadership; the other camp doesn't believe there are set characteristics that tie directly to leadership traits, capabilities, and gender.

Whichever side you fall on, I really don't care. But, I would staunchly argue there are, without a doubt, societal expectations and stereotypes of behavior traits for men, women, and leaders, and those gender norms have, and continue to, affect women.

Behavioral Expectations

A vast number of researchers and writers, supported by mainstream public opinion, agree: there are clear differences between expected and accepted styles and behaviors for males and females. Women are generally expected to act communally (or in ways traditionally considered "feminine") by showing warmth, compassion, cooperation, honesty, sympathy, helpfulness, nurturance, and sensitivity to others. Men, on the other hand, are generally considered to demonstrate agentic behaviors (or act with "masculine" qualities) by being ambitious, independent, assertive, competent, determined, decisive, and competitive.

Communal Behaviors:	Agentic Behaviors:
• Compassionate	• Assertiveness
• Nurturing	• Ambitious
• Helpful	• Determined
• Cooperative	• Competitive
• Sensitive	• Decisive

Studies show agentic traits are also considered to be characteristics most often associated with leadership—possibly because males have historically dominated leadership positions. As a result, this fine line can make it harder to distinguish between masculine qualities and those characteristics we typically expect leaders to demonstrate.

CHAPTER 8

Caught in the Middle

Unlike men in the same position, women leaders have to continue to walk the fine line between appearing incompetent and nice and competent but cold.

~ CORDELIA FINE

As women are increasingly moving up the ladder into roles and positions of authority traditionally held by men, the possibility of leadership behaviors being different for men than women has garnered more attention. As a result of this increase in power and positions, questions have surfaced regarding whether or not women lead in a different manner than men do.

Although there's general consensus that women encounter more challenges in achieving leadership roles, especially in male-dominated industries, there seems to be additional disagreement about how women act, or should act, once they gain these positions of authority (Eaglyl & Johannesen-Schmidt, 2001).

So, what *are* these leadership style differences between males and females? How are women leaders *supposed* to act, anyway? Really, it all goes back to agentic (masculine) and communal (feminine) behavioral expectations, which, by the way, are the factors leading to stereotypes and discrimination.

Stereotypes make it easy and convenient to label people or groups into categories, whether positive or negative. Any review of feminine and masculine traits must be grounded in a discussion of societal and cultural beliefs, roles, and rules connected to being either female or male. One of the criteria we're judged on when making a first impression is gender, and research has proven most people maintain assumptions about others based largely on gender-specific stereotypes (Barbuto & Gifford, 2010; Ely, 1995).

Stereotypes become an issue when these categories are used to supersede a woman's individual attributes. These stereotypes and beliefs don't get checked at the door when you get to work either; they overflow into the workplace and result in threats to the evaluation and advancement of others, more specifically women leaders. As a result, certain behaviors are deemed accepted, and even expected, based on the leader's gender. The outcome of these gender stereotypes is typically a strong, albeit invisible, barrier to women in leadership roles and their career progression.

These stereotypes, and the resulting bias, are generally underestimated. Don't get me wrong; I'm not saying men are the only ones who believe in stereotypes either. I presume we're all guilty in one form or another. But, research has proven that women are consistently reporting gender stereotypes as barriers to their advancement (Catalyst, 2007).

Imbedded in these ingrained beliefs are expectations of what women are like and how they're expected to behave. These stereotypes generally lead to people assuming women don't possess the qualities deemed necessary for effective leadership. This results in false perceptions and assumptions that women leaders don't have the traits and characteristics needed to effectively influence a company, when compared to men.

What's the difference between the ways men lead versus the ways women do? Study after study has confirmed: men are more often linked to leadership behaviors and traits than women (Eagly & Carli, 2007b). Female gender roles dictate that women are supposed to behave in communal ways, and leadership roles require leaders act agentically (Catalyst, 2007). Even though qualities such as ambition, competence, independence, and assertiveness are necessary for success, these characteristics are deemed less acceptable for women.

For example, researchers have concluded that both females and males are socialized to believe that males are more intelligent than females. Even little girls as young as age six are more likely to label little boys as "really, really smart" than they are to see their own gender's brilliance (Bian, Leslie, & Cimpian, 2017). As a result of such stereotypical beliefs, women leaders generally face a dilemma, as they're often left in precarious positions—a catch-22 (or commonly referred to as a double bind), if you will.

A double bind occurs when conflicting and contradictory expectations are made on someone, so that regardless of what demand is adhered to, the person's response is deemed incorrect—they can't win for losing. For example, if a female leader behaves in ways others perceive as too feminine, she's often criticized for not showing enough strength for a position of authority; she may be seen as behaving more "like a woman" than as a leader and risks being taken seriously. On the other hand, if a female leader behaves in ways that are more commonly considered masculine, she's seen as being unfeminine. These women are generally considered to be seen as more abrasive, and are often given the highly popular title of "bitch."

Females experience double binds from birth, and as we become older it seems they're compounded exponentially by personal experiences, beliefs, thoughts, relationships, and especially media portrayals of women. Stereotypes of females are everywhere you look—movies, television, music, advertising, the Internet, you name it. They're all around us.

Media and the bombardment of images are more than mere entertainment too; these sources teach, tell stories, convince, and shape lives, defining parameters about who women should be and how they should communicate and connect with others. How women are portrayed in media is generally negative and devaluing. Think of the different types of television programs you've watched. How many show strong, confident, educated women who have incredible leadership positions and act with integrity? Oh wait—there are none!

This barrage of unlimited female stereotypes plays directly into the double binds we experience. For example, girls and women are socialized with messages to act and behave in ways that are sexual; however, when they do, they're criticized at the same time for using their sexuality by garnering attention to advance their careers. As a result, females are depicted in the media as either being sex objects or that they have a brain—but God knows, we can't be both.

Women, especially leaders, are in precarious positions as these catch-22s affect how they express themselves, act, behave, the risks they take, and the choices they make (Holiday & Rosenberg, 2009). Although great strides have been made by females in academic and work circles, tremendous pressures continue to exist for girls and women to be kind, sweet, and nurturing, as opposed to being tough or competitive.

Because of this, girls learn early on to conceal hostility and anger as opposed to displaying these behaviors outwardly. As a result, this suppression of emotion comes at a considerable cost.

Women leaders are expected to fulfill their female gender role of being selfless, warm, and nurturing, while also behaving in congruence with leadership expectations of being competent, assertive, and dominant. When female leaders act more communally, then questions typically arise about their leadership competence; these leaders are usually seen as not being agentic enough.

On the other hand, women leaders who behave in a more agentic way may garner disapproval for lacking communal characteristics and traits. Because of these competing demands, women often reported they feel the need to outperform their male counterparts in an effort to be seen as equally competent (Eagly & Carli, 2007a).

Influence, which is defined as the ability or power to affect others' behavior or beliefs, is a requirement for effective leadership. Because of the impact of the double bind, however, it comes as no surprise that people may resist a woman's leadership, especially when the setting is masculine. Sometimes communal women face resistance because they're viewed as lacking competence, resulting in a lack of respect from their peers and subordinates.

Other women may demonstrate a more agentic style of leadership, resulting in people not liking them. Therefore, for females in leadership to successfully influence others and be liked and respected requires an often difficult, demanding balancing act (Eagly & Carli, 2007b).

Women may experience disparity in their career advancements and leadership as a result of gender differences, altering the course of their leadership development. Gender differences may lead to missed opportunities and advancements necessary for leadership skills and traits to develop. As a result, in an effort to attain workplace promotions, women leaders may feel it necessary to go to greater lengths than their male colleagues. This can include changes and adjustments to behaviors at work, which potentially can result in role conflict on the job.

Women are "emotional." Men are "passionate."

One woman talked about the differences in acceptance of female and male leaders when it comes to the double bind. "I have to say, I've seen men who are very emotional, but they don't call it emotional. Oh my gosh, it's not called emotional! It's called boisterous or passionate. It's so funny, there are some downright emotional men leaders, but they don't call it that. I think we just call it different things and accept it different ways. A woman being emotional in a meeting is completely not acceptable. Whereas the man being emotional, he's angry, he's passionate, he's irate…and that's okay."

Another female, a hospital CEO, talked of the journeys of others she's witnessed, with regard to the double bind they were in. "I see other women experience this, but I haven't, because I'm very tough-skinned. But I see other women failing because of the female thing of being emotional, being sensitive, and crying and getting their feelings hurt. I don't ever have that problem. I can hold my own, but from being a female peer and watching, I see that."

Have you ever had the experience of working with women who showed their emotions in meetings? Or really anywhere at work? I have, and I'll tell you—it makes people visibly uncomfortable and they don't know how to deal with it, even as females. And when tears happen in front of men, I see their eyes completely glaze over and they begin to fidget and look around like they're thinking, "Will someone please make it stop!"

I think we've all had tears at work, and we certainly cry for different reasons. Here's the differentiator and my advice: if you're crying out of compassion for a person or situation, that's one thing. To empathize or sympathize with someone and let that person know you care is an acceptable reason to show emotion. But crying out of frustration or because things aren't going your way is completely different.

Seriously, I know we've all had days where we get so frustrated or angry and don't know how to process the feelings we're experiencing. We are human, after all. But I suggest if you're in a moment where you feel the tears coming on, then it's best to excuse yourself and head straight for your office, the bathroom, a quiet place, outside, or your car and go regain your composure.

There's a time and a place for crying out of frustration, and a meeting is not an appropriate time or place. In fact, the workplace is just not the best place to shed tears from frustration or anger, period. Unfortunately, you'll lose a large amount of your hard-earned credibility by resorting to the water works, so do your best not to jeopardize that.

However, on the flip side, the opposite is also true. Women who tend to behave with more masculine traits (which, again, are most commonly connected to what people tend to view as expected for leadership), well sadly, these women are criticized too. When women demonstrate qualities that make them outwardly appear qualified for leadership positions, their competence ratings on performance reviews are equal to those of agentic men, but those women suffer backlash and social repercussions. They are seen as needing to lead by being less authoritative and needing to behave in a more "female" way.

"You have to sit at the table and cannot be emotional," one woman reported. "When I say emotional, I mean I have women colleagues, and a few of them are physicians, and they get so dramatic when they're sitting in meetings. That doesn't go well when they're sitting with the men. The men sit there and roll their eyes, you know? And I've seen female doctors have their meltdowns and yell and scream. There's one physician we have, and she's always so dramatic and emotional. It just doesn't go over well with the guys. As women, we need to be factual, we need to be prepared when it comes to meetings, know our data, and stick to our goal."

Women who behave agentically are generally considered socially deficient in comparison to their male counterparts. These women typically earn the not-so-coveted title of being a bitch. Lorraine Martinelle reported to Lean In.Org, "As editor I had to make tough decisions and unpopular choices. I had to let a few people go, and they resent me for it to this day. Being a woman, you're called the 'B' word if you put your foot down. A man would be respected as a leader if he did the things I did, but I got a lot of flak. I cried in front of my staff, I wish I hadn't, but I did. I was under a lot of pressure."

Another woman reported, "I'm very conscious of what I say and how I say it. And I don't think men have to think about that. I don't want to come across wrong, or be labeled a bitch. But I don't want certain things to be said or be done, you know? I don't tolerate people's ignorance very well."

I know this has been the experience I've encountered on my personal journey. When I was starting my company and new at leading teams, I had a difficult time managing my emotions under stress. My instinctive response wasn't to cry, but I did get upset and say things in a heated, upfront manner I knew I'd later regret. And then, every time, I'd have to go back and remedy the situation once I'd been able to think more clearly.

I'll never forget in the beginning when the company was growing, but I was still covering payroll with my credit cards. Needless to say I was dealing with immense amounts of stress. One day I came into the office from completing patient visits and I noticed my request from the previous day hadn't been fulfilled. Unfortunately I went ballistic on the newly hired receptionist. It wasn't pretty.

Thankfully she saw past my behavior and looked at my intent, knowing I was under a tremendous amount of pressure. She has stuck with me through the years, despite my shortcomings, and has moved through the ranks of the organization as we've continued to grow. We still look back on that day and laugh, but it wasn't funny at the time. I earned a nice, solid reputation of being a hard-to-work-for bitch for quite some time.

However, the lesson here in all of this is: in general, crying (out of frustration or anger) or being overly emotional in any way at the office are not recommended as strategies for career advancement. Do your best to remove your emotions from the situation and continue on. You have a job to do, so focus on that and your outcomes for success.

CHAPTER 9

Potential versus Performance

If you want something said, ask a man.
If you want something done, ask a woman.

~ Margaret Thatcher

Joan C. Williams, professor of law at the University of California and co-author of *What Works for Women at Work: Four Patterns Working Women Need to Know,* stated that men tend to be judged by their work potential; women are judged by their work performance. She believes women don't get promotions because supervisors think they're a little more of a risk than promoting a male. She stated that, in her experience, she has seen supervisors not promote women, justifying their decisions by saying, "We just have to see what she really has... it may be a little too early for her," whereas a man, on the other hand, he's already got the promotion.

Women often have difficulty creating their own, appropriate leadership style for themselves. A 2007 study of Fortune 1000 female executives found that 96 percent of them stated it was "vital" or "fairly imperative" to create a leadership style male managers are comfortable with. However, that in itself implies women aren't comfortable leading in a way that's authentic and genuine to themselves; they're obviously more concerned with how they'll be perceived as leaders than being able to lead in a manner consistent to their internal compass. Actually, it's pretty sad.

I have a friend who's employed at a clinic as a social worker. The clinic was staffed with all female social workers and the department head supervisor position was vacant. None of the other social workers, including my friend, were provided the opportunity to interview for the supervisory role, despite being employed by the company for several years. Instead, the home office hired a male psychologist to fill the vacancy so they could "add a little testosterone to the mix." Now, I know this is just one example, but these types of occurrences happen all the time where women aren't even considered to fill the void. Why do you think that is?

To become leaders, females must successfully make their way through the maze of obstacles and dead ends. In a perfect world, women and men would have similar leadership journeys; however, that's not the case. People typically have comparable views and beliefs about men and leaders but conflicting views of females in leadership (Schein, 2001). Hence the double bind.

Multiple books have been written offering advice for females on how to advance their careers. The problem, though, is the advice given is conflicting—and inauthentic. We experience invisible pressures against being authentic because of contradictory messages we receive about our ability to be beautiful, intelligent, assertive, competent, and a whole host of other qualities and attributes.

With regard to leadership and how females are encouraged to lead, two methods are typically promoted—to behave in a way that's overly feminine, or, alternatively, to act like a man. One of the problems I have with this advice, and suggesting that women in leadership should focus on how they come across to others, is that it diverts attention from the mission and purpose instead of concentrating on what needs to be accomplished.

Another problem I have with that is it doesn't help women develop their leadership skills based on their own personal, individual strengths. And who said there's only one way to effectively lead an organization, anyway?

There's a continued pervasive belief in business that women don't fit the criteria or image of what an ideal leader should look like (Catalyst, 2007). Because individuals have the tendency to view men as stereotypical leaders, female leadership behaviors are usually compared to male norms. Meaning, it's difficult, if not nearly impossible, for women to measure up.

"Even when 'feminine' leadership behaviors are perceived positively—such as when women are complimented for being team-oriented and sensitive to others' concerns—women's styles are still labeled as 'unique' and 'different' from the (presumed) leadership norm" (Catalyst, 2007, p. 9).

Unfortunately, here's the deal, and the double bind: when women express themselves outside of the "norm" of what's socially expected and deemed acceptable behavior for females, they experience negative responses from their peers. Women are stereotypically considered "emotional," and generally those emotions and responses are devalued and seen as being "hysterical." On the other hand, when a woman is void of showing emotion, she's also undervalued because she's not behaving in ways that are congruent with a stereotypical female.

Seriously, I'm not usually one to play the victim, but we're damned if we do, and doomed if we don't. The stereotypes and double binds that females experience and must maneuver through seemingly are enough to hold us back. But, wait! It gets better (do you hear the sarcasm?). Keep reading, though, because there's more hindering our leadership journeys and advancement than stereotypes and the double bind. Houston, we have even *more* problems.

CHAPTER 10

The Good Ol' Boys' Club

This issue of parity is not a women's issue. It's a societal issue that needs to be resolved by men and women.

~ STACEY ALLASTER

Although women have made great strides in gaining mid-level leadership positions in the past few decades, gender disparity remains in the upper levels of leadership and executive roles. More than 75 percent of CEOs include gender equality initiatives in their top ten business concerns, but gender statistics across the largest companies aren't changing.

In a recent study conducted by Lean In.Org and McKinsey, men in corporate America are promoted at rates 30 percent higher than their female counterparts in the early career stages. We've already touched briefly on one of the reasons why this disparity remains for female leaders by covering the leadership catch-22 and the double bind issue. Let's further this discussion by looking at how men contribute to the matter.

Ah, the good ol' boys... Men, especially white males, have been at the top of American organizational charts since the beginning of time. Women have only come into the working world since World War II. In 1900 the workforce was roughly 20 percent female. However, during WWII, the enlistment of so many men in the armed forces left gaping holes in the work force, systematically filled by women.

By 1945, nearly one in four married women was employed outside the home. But even as recently as the 1960s, the division of labor dictated that women should be homemakers and care for the kids while men went out and climbed the ladder of success as the sole breadwinners of the family.

Think back to how television shows like *Father Knows Best, Leave It to Beaver,* and even more recently as *The Brady Bunch* portrayed family life. Hell, even think of how in the 1980s, not that long ago, we had movies like *9 to 5* with the stereotypical secretary played by Dolly Parton. Men were the dominant leaders in the workforce and women were expected to be submissive—in both their roles at home and at work.

So how does that translate to the current working world of today? Not too long ago, men predominantly occupied the workforce and leadership ranks were *only* a man's playing field. When women began working, we started to play "their game" and we're all still learning to work together to figure out the rules. Men are learning to share their sandbox, if you will. And I give credit to those pioneers, men and women, who helped us pave the way on our own journeys.

I've seen, heard of, and been a gracious recipient of instances where men have gone out of their way to help me and other women advance. And to all of them who have, I'd like to personally thank them. We need more of you in our corner to help us navigate the maze of obstacles in this territory called work.

However, there are also a few of you men who aren't so thrilled to be sharing your toys; and those are the ones we'll refer to as the *good ol' boys' club.* Now hear me out, not all men are lumped into this category. But there are still some in the leadership ranks who go above and beyond their call of duty to convolute the paths for women and their attempts to advance their careers and themselves. And to you I say: shame on you.

The majority of women I spoke to discussed how they were negatively impacted by *some* of the men they encountered on their journeys of career progress. One participant spoke of her employer's initiative to assist with women's career advancement, but the committee spearheading the effort was a group of white males. When she tried to give input about diversification to the group and questioned the participants of the group about how long the initiative had been in place and how success was being measured, the committee laughed at her and brushed aside her comments.

Another woman spoke of her struggles and challenges trying to grow her career in west Texas but stated she was limited by the opportunities available to her because of gender. "Without a doubt, my biggest obstacle in my career development has been because I live in a good ol' boys area. I've lived here for quite some time, and as a partner in a company in a male dominated industry, my challenge has been developing business when I'm typically not even invited to the table because I'm female."

Several of the participants spoke specifically about the networks men have and the struggle women have when trying to compete. "The good ol' boys' club is one of the biggest challenges. They promote each other. They have very big egos, and as a female you have to work harder. They just have a different personality. They're all about themselves, very egotistical, fists against their chests. And if a woman was out there doing the same, I feel men would laugh at her for being over-aggressive, loud, and obnoxious. And it's a very big obstacle because the men will always stick together."

Another woman spoke of an experience she'd encountered on her career climb, stating, "In my first homecare job, you were not a manager if you were female. There were female schedulers, but even the bonuses were different. You could be on the same level as someone else but the males made 10 percent bonus and the females made a flat bonus. It was obvious, yes, very obvious; the females were treated much differently. It was very stressful, and I did make comments. There were certain people who didn't like me. I wasn't always liked, but I did my job."

Many women talked about generational changes they foresee with regard to leadership. One woman said, "I haven't seen gender issues where I am now, but I did in my prior workplace. From the older regime, not the younger, but they're also on their way out. The women executives had to prove themselves more, but I also see that leadership retiring and leaving and going into emeritus positions. I think in the next five to ten years we're going to have a very different environment."

Another woman referenced her experiences in the workforce and stated she was hopeful the good ol' boys' club would be shutting down in the not-so-distant future due to Millennials gaining ground in upper organizational ranks.

Is the wave of Millennial leaders (also called Gen Y) going to bring about change, enlightenment, and equality for women in the workforce? In 2013 *Time* magazine envisioned Millennials as the savior for gender differences, concluding they were "more accepting of differences...in everyone" (Stein, 2013). Later that year, *The Atlantic* conveyed the Millennial generation cared more about gender equality than racial equality, stating, "There are no inherently male or female roles in society" (Winograd & Hais, 2013). In 2014, a generational expert blogger reported in the *Huffington Post* that Gen Y men are most likely going to view women as equals (Turner, 2014).

As evidenced by the predictions, one would assume our heroes have arrived. Are Millennials going to save us? Before we put all of our faith in this generation, let's look at some more recent data.

According to a February 2016 study published by the National Institutes of Health, Gen Y male biology college students consistently overestimated the abilities of their male classmates when compared to the women (Grunspan et al., 2016). Even as the semester progressed, the men's inaccurate assessment of their peers' abilities increased in spite of obvious evidence of the women's exceptional performance. In all of the biology classes studied, a male was believed to be the top-ranking student, even when a female had superior grades. However, in contrast, the women students polled didn't have a bias, as they were accurate assessors of their peers' performance.

> *Men's inaccurate assessment of their peers' abilities increased in spite of obvious evidence of the women's exceptional performance.*

Although this is just one account of continued bias among the Millennial generation, there's more confirmation that we can't put all our eggs in their young little baskets. In a 2014 survey of more than 2,000 adults, Harris Poll found that Millennial males were not as open to accepting female leaders as older males were (Pershing, 2016). For instance, only 39 percent of Gen Y men reported being supportive of women being CEOs of Fortune 500 companies, versus 61 percent of men aged sixty-five and older.

Even when considering the role of president of the United States, 35 percent of Millennial men said they'd be supportive of a woman whereas 57 percent of men in the older group reported they would be. The numbers were 41 percent versus 65 percent for women being engineers, and 43 percent compared to 64 percent for women being U.S. senators.

In 2014 a shred of hope was found when Harvard Business School conducted a massive survey of MBA graduates and found Millennial males were more likely than previous generations to predict their wives would have equal careers. The men also predicted their wives would be less likely to take the sole responsibility for child-rearing. However, that hope dissipated when the researchers discovered the gap between the beliefs of the two Millennial genders remained large.

Approximately 75 percent of the women surveyed believed their careers would be equally as important as their spouses; however, half the men held assumptions that their own careers would come first. With regard to family responsibilities, less than 50 percent of the women polled thought they would manage the majority of the childcare, but 67 percent of the males believed their wives would handle that duty. So, still think there are no prescribed gender roles, Millennial males? Evidently it's not what was said when it came right down to it (Ely, Stone, & Ammerman, 2014).

Considering the data, I beg to differ with the claim that Millennial men will be our knights in shining armor because they come into the workforce viewing women as equals. In fact, if something isn't done to change their beliefs and biases toward women, this age group of males who are quickly ascending up the corporate ladder may actually block current strides to gain equality.

But, just for grins, let's say they were our saviors; let's consider a future hypothetical. In a perfect world, let's say all men begin to see the value in women's contributions and their leadership styles. That would alleviate the issue and we'd be able to climb the corporate ladder without resistance, right? Ha! Not so fast. I hate to break it to you, ladies, but we have enemies within the troops.

CHAPTER 11

Women: Enemies in the Camp

I see actresses just a little bit ahead of me who really saw women as their enemy... Now, that's certainly not true. You might be envious of a part you didn't get but it's switched to understanding that you need women as allies and that we're stronger together, not divided.

~ Susan Sarandon

One of the biases I began my research with was that men, particularly the good ol' boys, were responsible for blocking women from gaining ground in leadership positions. You know, like they didn't want us playing on their turf or something. As you can see, there were definitely instances where that has, and continues to occur. However, according to my research results, this level of discrimination wasn't solely coming from males in the workforce.

More often than men being discussed as the culprits for blocking women's success, however, *women* were identified as responsible for holding back women from advancing. Sadly, when women believe and engage in their own stereotypical female behaviors, they're often participants in perpetuating their own oppression.

Interestingly enough, it appears that when people feel less

worthy than others or inadequate in their own skin, they tend to act in the opposite way; they behave by treating others badly and act as if they believe they're superior to others. As a result, women hold themselves and other females back from leadership positions by betraying, hurting, condemning, backstabbing, and excluding other females.

"While workplace studies show women are routinely underestimated compared to men, we don't give much credence to the fact that women hampering other women is also to blame" states *Washington Post* journalist Selena Rezvani (2012). While it's not pleasant to consider how women have the tendency to hold each other back or tear each other apart, unfortunately this behavior exists way too often.

Many of the interviewees, more than 80 percent, spoke of having encountered women who either demonstrated how not to behave or prevented them from advancing on their career journeys. The more women I questioned, the more it became clear these instances were not specific to one particular industry. This pervasive problem is rampant, and it needs to be addressed if we're ever going to gain equal pay, leadership, and equality in the workplace.

How Not to Behave

Stories were repeatedly shared of females behaving in ways we shouldn't emulate. These recollections ranged from personal experiences of situations happening to the participants to passive examples of seeing instances occur to others. Many spoke of witnessing other females using their femininity to get ahead, gossiping, backstabbing, lying, or seemingly going out of their way to sabotage another woman's success.

Mei Xu, Chesapeake Bay Candle Chief Executive Officer and founder, relayed, "It is not only men who may sometimes have issues with a woman business leader—sometimes it is also women. I don't know exactly why but it seems that some women can be afraid of other women who are successful or smart" (Rezvani, 2010b).

Now, I'm not naïve enough to think women are the only ones capable of this type of behavior and men don't hold other men down, but men aren't screaming from the rooftops about advancement and equal pay. Conducting ourselves this way is dangerous and damaging to our gender's credibility. Ladies, if we ever want to have the honor of leading other people at work, we have to act like leaders now!

Story after story, I heard women reflect about how other females not only behave poorly at work, but also become downright hateful and nasty. One participant, a hospital CEO said, "I would say I had six or seven folks who have definitely guided me along the way. In certain instances, in what to do, and in some cases I've learned what not to do by a few folks. But what was interesting was I was asked who my female mentors were in my career, and I realized I didn't have that many. Those were mainly the instances of where I learned what not to do." Ouch.

Other situations were relayed about women using their femininity to get ahead. One respondent recalled her time in medical sales: "In that profession, you had to use all your feminine characteristics and capabilities, because you had to schmooze the doctor and you had to get in to see him. You had to be pretty frisky and flirtatious, and that's why I didn't succeed in it."

Multiple women discussed how they witnessed fellow female colleagues attempt to gain attention or even promotions by dressing provocatively. Interestingly, however, typically flirtation and risqué dress did not result in advancement, but rather wound up with the person being subject of conversation around the water cooler.

"What's done in attempts to get recognition and attention actually results in the opposite effect," Tara Hooper, a Dallas area professional image consultant, said. "Women don't realize when they dress seductively they're sending the opposite message. They won't get the respect and advancement, or the female friendships they're seeking, because they won't be taken seriously."

A friend of mine, who works in a large accounting firm, had ample to say about women and the way some appear to attempt to advance their careers by dressing provocatively. She said, "There are categories, really. There's the first group, who are the ones who dress that way because they don't care. Then you have the second group, who dress that way and are intentional, but tacky about it. And then you have the third group, who are intentional in a cool, Marilyn Monroe kind of way. But really, it backfires on all of the groups because what they don't realize is that they all polarize themselves from other women." Interesting, though. Do you think they don't realize, or do you think they realize and really just don't care?

Encounters of the Dangerous Kind

Many women discussed either a lack of mentors available or their experiences with women who had directly impacted their career journeys—negatively. When I asked about having experiences with female mentors, sadly, a handful even laughed. How could I suggest such a thing even existed! One respondent stated, "When you get into the upper echelons of healthcare administration, there aren't many females. The ones I've encountered haven't always been someone you want to emulate. So while they were mentors, they weren't always positive mentors."

The most memorable response to whether or not a participant in the study had a female mentor came from a hospital CEO, who replied, "Mentors? I haven't had mentors; I have had *tormentors*! Most of them were women. Nurses eat their young, they're kind of like sharks. When I became a nurse and was being trained, certain nurses would leave parts of the education out of how to do a procedure or how to set up a room. They wanted to be the hero in the physician's eyes. It should be about building relationships and not hiding information. But it happened a lot. I felt it very strongly when I was a clinician. But when I got into management it didn't stop there with nurses. It was many females in management."

Kellie McElhaney, a professor in California, told Lean In.Org about her experience. She was conducting research to prove that companies with more women on their boards had greater social, environmental, and governance performance. McElhaney relayed that she wrote about her research and presented it for the first time to a group of female CEOs, presidents, and board members in New York. She recalled, "They tore it to shreds. They didn't want to be associated with anything other than hard business returns, and certainly not the soft stuff of environment or community. They insisted they didn't see any difference between male and female business leaders. It was the last audience from whom I expected such staunch criticism."

Why would women want to be so cruel, to anyone, let alone to one another? I'm not saying offer fake support, but to go above and beyond to bully a peer is unnecessary. So, let's look at the root causes of why some women demonstrate this behavior.

CHAPTER 12

The Mean Girl Syndrome

Mean girls go far in high school.
Kind women go far in LIFE.

~ Mandy Hale

According to a 2014 survey by the Workplace Bullying Institute, woman-on-woman harassment is on the rise. Yes, you read that correctly. An actual institute exists to track and report workplace bullying. How sad is that? Women reportedly bullied other women colleagues in 68 percent of the cases (Workplace Bullying Institute, 2014).

There are several theories of why certain women seem to be consumed by female competitiveness, but the point remains: particular women attempt to level their playing field by resorting to being cold and hurtful to anyone who crosses their path. I will admit I, too, have been guilty of judging women without cause, or with what I justified as a legitimate reason. But what are the root causes of this cannibalistic behavior? Basically, it happens to stem from the double binds and ways we're socialized as females, especially how we're taught to deal with aggression.

Some mean girls never grow up.

When you boil it down, hurtful, harmful behavior occurs among girls as a result of their experiences of feeling inadequate with themselves. It appears this type of behavior stems from fear and anxiety and a deep-seated desire for acceptance. This inadequacy, which develops over time due to societal expectations and media influences, leaves some girls with feelings of self-hatred when dealing with competitive situations.

Unfortunately, though, some mean girls never grow up. They don't play by the rules and bring their childish antics they learned on the playground into work as they develop into mean women. Where's the unity of sisterhood? Let's take a look at the contributing factors.

Socialization and Aggression

Girls are raised and socialized into many double binds that deter them from outwardly expressing their feelings of anger. Girls and women are taught not to be competitive in our culture. In general, females in American society are discouraged from feelings and actions of being independent, ambitious, assertive, and aggressive—the same qualities leaders must have to be successful; however, these attributes are acceptable, and even encouraged for males.

Girls are taught to refrain from conflict, and learn from an early age that overtly displaying aggressive behaviors are frowned upon. As a result, girls learn to express their feelings of anger, conflict, and competition quite differently than boys. Unfortunately, we have to deal with those feelings somehow, and the result becomes indirect aggression (eye rolling and disapproving, dirty looks) and all kinds of deceitful and manipulative behaviors—overtly and covertly.

This subject and resulting double bind is convoluted. Females often are highly competitive with one another over concerns such as beauty, intellect, achievement, and even attention from males. But, because of how we're socialized and the fact that we aren't "supposed" to be competitive, we don't discuss this competition with anyone; in fact, most women deny this competition has any significance to them, mostly because we're taught to be humble and not prideful.

However, when a woman compares herself to other women, and believes they have succeeded in an area in which she falls short, (which, ladies, we probably do multiple times a day) the pain is visceral; it feels almost unbearable.

On the other hand, males typically grow up in teams, often playing sports, where they learn the value of working together for a unified goal. When they get angry they demonstrate their frustrations and anger with physical aggression; and when they can't take someone out that way, they resort to verbal assaults. There is comparatively, for the most part, limited behind-the-back drama and deception. Boys (and men) let you know where you stand—because they tell you.

A factor that contributes to women holding one another down is women are internally dealing with insecurities. Insecure behavior and comments come out in a variety of ways, from waiting for the other woman to leave the room to attempting to sabotage her with a whisper. "Many of us have witnessed the man who comments on a woman's hotness just as she leaves the room. But what about the woman who criticizes another's appearance (Did you see what she was wearing in there?) or frowns on a woman's unapologetic use of power (Just who does she think she is?)?" Rezvani writes (2012).

In the book *Mean Girls, Meaner Women*, by Drs. Erika Holiday and Joan Rosenberg, the coauthors wrote, "Self-hatred is the key link between girls' early hurtful behavior toward each other and women who suppress other women. A woman with a strong sense of self and high self-esteem is much less likely to hurt others."

Media's Impact

Without a doubt, the demands placed upon females have changed over the past decade. Whether it's a conscious decision or not, girls resort to handling their feelings of competition and aggression based on what's portrayed in the media. Mass media (including advertising, print, TV, movies, computer, Internet, etc.) acts as a source for socializing society, and our society, promotes and supports a culture of women being aggressive and hostile toward one another.

Sadly, media is a reflection of our current society and also has the power to influence our future. Media in our culture has made a fortune on marketing, exploiting, and sensationalizing women hurting and betraying other women. "Reality" TV is the worst, but whether these programs are real or not, they perpetuate the stereotypes, marginalization, and oppression of women by affecting social norms—making hateful, despicable, hurtful betrayal and behavior between women acceptable. How could we not be influenced when we consider the effects of repeated exposure to this type of behavior and our own self-image?

Although there are only a handful of women in movies and TV portrayed as positive role models in leadership roles, there are a much greater number of shows that denigrate women. Females are often placed in roles where their hostility toward other women is depicted center-stage. In fact, the bigger the conflict, hurt, humiliation, aggression, drama, "cat-fighting," and division among women, the larger the focus. It baffles me how grown adults can act this way, or how this behavior could be considered anything remotely close to entertaining!

A high sense of self-esteem and the belief that we're free to be our authentic selves is difficult, as we're influenced by the daily inundation of media images. When we believe what's being shown in media images is real, and not altered or staged, then our own personal reality becomes greatly transformed.

As a result, we tend to view the real world as comparable, acceptable, and expected to what's viewed in the media.

The resulting absence of personal power, security in ourselves, and ability to self-regulate our behaviors are overwhelming, as women often turn this aggression and anger inward first; the ensuing self-hatred is the foundation of the harmful actions with which females treat each other.

> *What is deemed acceptable behavior in media has*
> *a spillover impact on how we treat one another.*

Women, how much lower will we allow ourselves to be portrayed? How much worse can it get? The issue is this: what's deemed acceptable behavior in media has a spillover impact on how we treat one another, whether we realize it or not. And it's not just us but our future generations. To what magnitude are we going to allow our actions and behaviors to decline by promoting and supporting such vile treatment of one another?

CHAPTER 13

Working Together

*If your actions create a legacy that inspires
others to dream more, learn more, do more and
become more, then, you are an excellent leader.*

~ DOLLY PARTON

We all know the stories of women not supporting each other, but there are also stories of women building each other up and being strong allies at work. I want you to hear me out—I'm not perpetuating the belief that women are all evil and conniving. I've had several supportive, positive female relationships, so I know firsthand we have the capacity to lift each other up. If we work together as a collective team we can go much further, and faster, in leveling the playing field.

I believe when we start supporting each other on this journey of career advancement, we have the capacity to take over the horizons of leadership. We have the intelligence, intuition, and skill to do it. Now, we just have to act like the leaders we want to be known as so we can all benefit.

Transformational Leadership: Changes on the Horizon

Leadership and the desire to know what makes leaders

successful have gained attention across the globe. What can be agreed upon, though, is that leadership can be somewhat difficult to define and study. The characteristics of a successful leader have changed and evolved over time. But the good news is there's a popular consensus that a distinct female leadership style exists.

Although early models of leadership focused mainly on hierarchy, more recent models have transitioned to focusing on methods that are behaviorally based, placing more value and greater emphasis on the study of successful interpersonal skills. Gone are the days of "do as I say, not as I do" leadership.

Research has shown women and men typically demonstrate different leadership styles. A closer look at nearly 50 studies found women leaders, in general, have a tendency to lead in a more transformational way than men. Female leaders were also seen as engaging in rewarding behaviors more frequently than males, even though this happens to be a characteristic of transactional leadership.

Men were characterized as behaving in styles more in alignment with transactional and laissez-faire (hands-off) leadership, demonstrating behaviors like correction and disciplinary actions. Overall, women were viewed as leading in a more collaborative and participative way than men.

In 1998 Carless, a researcher, conducted a study describing leadership styles and behaviors through the lens of transformational leadership, a term coined by J. V. Downton in 1978. According to Bass and Riggio (2006), transformational leaders are described as inspiring and stimulating followers to achieve extraordinary results through mentorship, coaching, and support.

These leaders go beyond setting simple agreements and exchanges with their followers and peers. Transformational leaders successfully achieve powerful results by demonstrating at least one of the following four descriptors: idealized influence, inspirational motivation, intellectual stimulation, and individualized consideration (Bass & Riggio, 2006).

According to Carless' findings (1998), both males and females reported that women demonstrated a more transformational leadership style than males, displaying traits such as participative decision-making, showing consideration for others, demonstrating nurturing behaviors, and exuding charisma. Carless concluded that, in general, female leaders were described as being more inclusive and participative, whereas their male counterparts were perceived as being controlling, directive, and task-oriented.

Carless attributed these findings to her belief that leadership development for females is a socialization process, stating that women are innately drawn to relational leadership behaviors and skills that appear to be most in line with a transformational leadership style. An additional study validated these differences, suggesting women in leadership roles appeared to more highly value the relational components of their positions more than it seemed men did (Boatwright & Forrest, 2000).

As leadership studies have shown, communal characteristics such as engaging in teamwork and collaboration, offering support, and listening have been emphasized as important traits for strong leaders. Women who show these types of characteristics, or even other communal characteristics, have the potential to reach higher level leadership ranks in their companies.

Career rewards and advancements are there for women who lead authentically to their true styles, if their true styles are to build others up and not to cut others down; I encourage you, don't change your leadership style to "lead like a man." That's such a dangerous message. I have heard women, and have seen books, that encourage females to change their leadership styles to lead like men, and it bothers me to no end. Staying true to your core characteristics will decrease your chances of feeling like you're caught in the double bind.

Transformational leadership, which research has shown more women demonstrate, is considered a greater, increasingly effective style for leading organizations in the 21st century.

So what does all this mean? Well, the short of it is this: transformational leadership, which research has shown more women demonstrate, is considered a greater, increasingly effective style for leading organizations in the 21st century. Because leadership talent is vital, and great leadership is rare, companies can't afford to not capitalize on any division of the talent pool. Gender stereotypes and bias have to be addressed head on so leadership talent is identified and utilized.

Regardless of how much women have accomplished or their levels of education, skill, qualifications, or leadership training, if companies don't address gender stereotypes and bias, they're going to continue to miss out in hiring and promoting exceptional talent.

But more than that, ladies, we have to stop behaving like mean girls in junior high and start acting as the grown-ups we are. We're asking for more opportunities as leaders and equal pay, but we're sabotaging our group's efforts when we stab each other in the back and hold each other down. *We* are a *team*. We'll all be more successful, have better opportunities for pay, and more chances for advancement when we acknowledge the power of standing arm in arm, as opposed to being back to back. When we start holding our heads high and helping one another, the good ol' boys won't have a chance to keep us down.

Company Culture Dictates Leadership

Because of environmental and organizational changes and demands put on teams, leaders have to take primary roles in their companies. The days of passive leadership are gone; today's leaders need to be ready, willing, and able to meet the changing needs of their industry. As organizations become increasingly complex, more emphasis will be put on leaders of all levels to accomplish goals effectively. High-level leaders are needed to be capable of motivating, encouraging, and inspiring their teams.

Organizational culture has a direct relationship, whether positive or negative, to the career progress of the females employed. The culture of a company isn't some distant, untouchable "thing" that's out there—rather it's the tone set by the people and leaders employed by the organization. Women who achieved success in their careers attributed part of their accomplishments to having a supportive organization dedicated to the success and advancement of women.

For one workplace in particular, what made this organization different was its commitment to its core value of making it the best place to work; and it didn't just talk about it either. This company has pillars of leadership that reward employees for serving as role models for all behavioral standards, including making no excuses for behaviors.

In other highly successful organizations, characteristics that attribute to positive company culture include leaders who teach others to lead, not acting or responding from a place of fear but of genuine support to encourage and see others grow. These leaders also keep a positive attitude and value their employees and their opinions, asking their teams to derive solutions to problems instead of top-down leadership. These companies ensure employees are committed to the overall satisfaction and morale of the organization, and allow for continuous and two-way feedback.

The point in giving descriptions of positive organizational cultures is because if that's the kind of place you want to work, that's the way you have to act. I hear people all the time complaining about their company not supporting or valuing them, but they aren't behaving in ways that warrant being supported and valued. And, another thing and then we'll move on—last I checked, if you're employed in an organization that doesn't respect and support you, then I'm pretty sure you aren't chained to the desk. You have the power and ability to leave! And when you're interviewing for another job, research the company before you accept a position. You can find tons of information online (think LinkedIn or Glassdoor) and see what their employees say about the organization and the culture. Don't stay in a place where you don't feel wanted.

CHAPTER 14

The Arsenal in Your Pocket

Succeeding in business is all about making connections.
~ RICHARD BRANSON

If women are to gain access to higher-level ranks of leadership, then we're going to have to start helping each other get there. According to recent research, one of the biggest reasons women aren't being promoted is because those at higher levels don't help others get ahead. From what we've discussed thus far, that probably doesn't come as a shock, but shame on them!

How many times have we heard other women voice the erroneous belief that because they had to learn the hard way, so should someone else? I hear stories of this happening all the time and it's infuriating to me. With that sort of mentality and keeping each other down, we'll never be successful in advancing to the top.

Unfortunately, too many females at the top deal with "value threat" which causes them to not want to give back and help other women (Lepore, 2014). A friend of mine experienced this at her last place of employment, and went on to start her own company as a result. She recounts, "The VP of my department hired me as the director to eventually replace her and bring more professionalism to the team. But as I continued to fall into the owner's favor, she had issues with being 'replaced' and no longer being his favorite. It was so obvious and frustrating. At forty years old I felt like I was back in middle school."

Women need to be—and have access to—more supportive, skilled leaders who are willing to strengthen them at all levels. They'd benefit by seeking out advisors, both male and female, who can help them see their potential and work toward career advancement. If we were beneficial in other women's advancement and gave back to others by supporting younger women who are currently navigating the challenges of climbing the corporate ladder, we could conquer the world—not just the boardroom.

Being a mentor or sponsor to those who are coming behind you in the organizational ranks is critical for women to engage in as leaders. I encourage you to advance your personal growth, even if people aren't lined up at your door offering to help.

Identifying and building your network is critical. Internal networks as well as external contacts are invaluable, not just to growing your career, but to having a group of associates you can go to for professional and personal reasons. Your network should include people who will mentor as well as sponsor you, and there's a difference. Although mentors and sponsors act in differing roles, their primary function is to give you support and guidance on your career journey. Here's how they're different.

Building a Team

Think of a mentor as someone who acts as your advisor, someone you can go to for advice and guidance. He or she isn't your coach or advocate, but will provide guidance for your personal and professional growth. A mentor-mentee relationship generally starts as a friendship, but doesn't always have to. Your mentor needs to be someone with a vested interest in you and your success, like your personal cheerleader who will shoot straight with you.

Your mentor needs to offer wisdom and knowledge to you, as someone who happens to have less experience than he or she does. Overall, a mentor is a person who provides support as a private sounding board for the mentee when dealing with convoluted, complex situations.

Mentors can be internal or external to your current organization. When you find people you respect and want them to mentor you (who aren't already your friends), don't ask them to be your mentor (it's as awkward as the boy in 7th grade was when he asked you for your first kiss). Instead, ask them how you can support them. Find ways to help them and be in their corner when they need something. They may or may not need anything, but it will make an impression that you're offering to be an advocate for them.

Find out if they're involved in any volunteer activities or sit on any boards; ask if there's a cause near and dear to their heart you could support. After the relationship has been developed, I suggest having a conversation like this, "I really admire you, your work ethic, and your integrity. I'd be grateful for the opportunity to learn more from you about your career journey and ways you have succeeded, as well as ways that might not have gone as planned. Would it be possible to meet for an hour once every other month?"

You don't have to use my words, but I'd say something similar to that effect; having that conversation is generally much better than outright asking someone to be your mentor, as that can result in an uncomfortable, awkward silence.

The Concept of Sponsorship

Having a workplace sponsor is a relatively new term, but the concept has been around for ages. A sponsor in business is someone who looks out for you at work when you need more visibility and uses his or her influence with those with more seniority to advocate for you. They let the "powers that be" know your work performance and ethics are solid and they go to bat for you when necessary, such as when top roles become available. Although not always someone you have a close, personal relationship with, sponsors can still give advice and feedback to you, because they believe in you and want to see you excel.

According to research, sponsorship appears to be even more beneficial than mentorship for the women workers who risk getting stuck in the middle. This is due in part because sponsorship, with the right connection, can offer you high-level contacts, broader perspectives when receiving feedback, and provide you with assignments that are designed to stretch you and advance your career.

Because sponsors speak up for you and are a valuable resource, don't take the relationship for granted. These executives are risking their name and reputation by supporting you and your career desires. For everyone's sake, including your own, ensure you demonstrate your value when given the chance. In other words, do your best, shine brightly, and don't disappoint.

CHAPTER 15

Expand Your Horizons

I never dreamed about success. I worked for it.

~ Estée Lauder

Are you, or have you been, in a situation where you're dealing with challenges at work because of your gender? There are ways to successfully navigate this part of the maze; don't give up. Rise above the circumstance, hold your head high, and don't give in to the attempts at sabotage or the games others play.

I recommend you diversify your activities outside of the four walls at work. One participant spoke of how she was employed in a good ol' boys' club and felt like it was time to move on. She became active in industry networks, at the chapter and regional levels, which led to engaging at the national board level for the past year. The connections she made were powerful and provided her the opportunity to find a better working environment. "I made the decision to rise above the situation and I used it as my motivation," she recalls. "I was challenged, but I didn't stay challenged. I looked beyond the circumstances. And now, I speak nationally for different organizations, I've been published, and I'm in different networks across the nation."

Another participant who dealt with men's network at her

previous employer used it as inspiration to work as an independent consultant for other healthcare providers; yet another female opened her own healthcare organization.

Kellie McElhaney recounted her experience to Lean In.Org when she told her peers in the academia and banking worlds she was going to focus on gender issues and how companies do better when they diversify top-level leadership. Her peers discouraged her, stating she'd face career suicide. McElhaney was motivated to keep going, realizing she was on a critical path. And she was. Her dedication to gender equality resulted in her creating an entirely new MBA course on women and business which, much to her surprise, filled up with men and women.

So maybe you aren't feeling the pull to change employers, start your own company, or write a college curriculum. That's okay! There are still ways you can make a difference right where you are.

First, I encourage you to help other women at work by being there for them, and not just to celebrate their successes or be a shoulder in disappointing times. We should all strive to create healthy relationships and show others they can count on us.

For example, I was talking to my friend Ali recently; she recounted a situation where her newly appointed supervisor, Sara, made it her personal mission to make my friend's life a living hell. Ali made the mistake of asking for clarification on a policy being rolled out, but she happened to ask in a group meeting. Apparently Sara considered Ali's question to be an act of insubordination and refused to support Ali's promotion from her prior supervisor.

In retaliation, Sara told the home office Ali was deficient in her training and insisted Ali go back through four months of training and jumping through hoops to prove she was qualified for the supervisory role. When Ali finally got her promotion and was transferred out of Sara's department she could have very easily been bitter and resentful; however, she chose to be a bigger person and not play Sara's games.

Karma always has a way of making the rounds, though, because Sara was in a bind and needed help on a project. Guess who came to her rescue? You got it—Ali! She chose to not let anger and revenge get the better of her. And if you're in a similar situation, you have that choice too.

Here are just a few ways I suggest that you, too, can support other women in the workplace. First, stop the gossip, betrayal, and backstabbing. Seriously, put an end to the junior high ways and don't associate with anyone who engages in that behavior. Rise above it; you're so much better.

Next, when those around you (at work or otherwise) characterize women as being aggressive, dominant, bossy, or even go so far as to call them bitches, challenge it by asking if they'd have the same opinion if they were discussing a man. Or, if you're having a negative response to a female co-worker, ask yourself the same question. Give your peers the benefit of the doubt and consider the possibility that she's just doing her job.

Part of the problem is that both men and women continue to perpetuate the double standard females face by categorizing strong, confident women as negative, as if somehow they're behaving in the wrong. Women, we have to begin asserting ourselves if we're to be taken seriously.

Which brings about my next point: ignite a spirit of unity and collaboration at work by being someone who encourages and supports others. It's no shock, I'm sure, that we're already on an uneven playing field at work. Research even shows the bias is so bad that just by changing the applicant's name on a resume to a man's name from a woman's name boosts the likelihood the candidate will be hired by 61 percent (Steinpreis, Anders, & Ritzke, 1999).

Seriously, it's that bad. But when you consider how we're

portrayed and how we often treat each other, it's not surprising that we're overlooked for positions of higher authority; I wouldn't want to deal with the drama either! Because of the fact that our abilities are often underestimated, we have to work harder to demonstrate our value and prove we're as capable, if not more, than our male counterparts.

I even read that women get interrupted more often, by both women and men, and are given credit for their ideas less often (Hancock & Rubin, 2015). So, it's no wonder that sadly, we internalize that message and begin to doubt our own abilities and worth.

We work harder to demonstrate our value and prove we're as capable, if not more, than our male counterparts.

CHAPTER 16

Making a Difference

Many women live like it's a dress rehearsal.
Ladies, the curtain is up and you're on.

~ Mikki Taylor

Let's look at the bright side. We have the potential to make a difference. When you're in a conversation, ensure you let others have the floor. And if a woman is speaking and you notice she's interrupted, interject and say you want to hear what she was saying.

Also, if you observe a co-worker taking credit for the thoughts or ideas of someone else, publicly remind your peers by saying, "That's a great idea. I know Dianne thought of it before, but I'm glad you brought it up again." When you promote your female peers, not only do they benefit, but you'll be seen as a leader.

And while we're talking about leading, I suggest you look for ways to encourage other women to take on those projects or positions for which they feel they aren't ready. As a result, you're then able to help boost their confidence. When a co-worker says she's not equipped for a new role or assignment, remind her what she's been able to achieve thus far. If we don't get support to go out on a limb and try new things, then we'll never grow, develop, and see our potential.

Employer mentorship programs for women with advancement potential can help keep female talent engaged in their current organizations. Employers and leaders are encouraged to ask women with high potential if they're interested in advancement and make attempts to support them on their career journeys. Ask them what they need to be successful, as we all have different drivers and motivators.

One of the best ways to lead others and give back is to be a mentor or sponsor. Be the person you wish you'd had on your career journey. One of the participants, a chief nursing officer, recalled her experience with the woman she identified as her biggest mentor, "I appreciated her style. I appreciated that when we had our meetings, she wouldn't make me come to her office, but she'd come to mine. She was no-nonsense, she knew the business, and knew the hospital inside and out. She had the respect of everyone, and you couldn't pull any crap with her. She didn't sugarcoat anything, but you always knew where you stood with her."

Which brings me to another suggestion on how you can support your female colleagues—give them direct, honest, constructive criticism (even when it's difficult). Research has shown that women generally receive more generic and less helpful feedback than men. Comments females hear are typically filled with more "fluff" and are less measurable, like "Great job!" or, "You need to communicate more."

This feedback is vague and makes any efforts to improve seem like an ambiguous shot in the dark. If you give clear, direct feedback such as, "Hey, great job in the meeting standing up and speaking out for the new project. Your insight on the budget for next year was spot on." Or even, "I'd like it if you communicated your frustration about the project to me so we can talk about it and work out the differences. I know you're under a tight deadline, but if we work together as a team, then we can help each other ensure we are both successful." Or something similar to those examples. Make your feedback such that whatever you say is specific, measurable, actionable, and repeatable by the person receiving it.

Self-reflection and awareness can be difficult, but they're the only way we can change the story—for ourselves and for those who follow. It's a gift to yourself and the results can be game changers. If you've previously experienced pain, then analyze the source of that hurt. Have you been the recipient of hurtful actions or words? Have you been the attacker? If you truly want your relationships with other women to be different, take the first step, start where you are, and do it now—there's no time like the present.

If you've treated others poorly—overtly or covertly—take some time to reflect on why; also examine what you got out of that behavior in return. How are you able to turn those situations around and work more collaboratively to get what you want? If you're still working with women you've hurt, be bold and brave and sincerely apologize. Consider seeking professional help if you're still engaging in this behavior. Further attacks on other women are really attacks on yourself. So stop.

Obviously conflicts and situations of disagreement will naturally arise in relationships. Making a commitment to end mean and aggressive behavior doesn't equate to not being angry. It means you'll deal with those feelings differently. The best way to resolve current and future discord is to speak the truth in love—directly but with compassion, without saying biting, hurtful things. Put a stop to harmful, undermining betrayal.

As women begin to feel and express anger, hurt, competition, jealousy, disappointment, or aggression in more healthy manners, the result will be less damaging and hurtful behaviors between women. So, feel it, express it to the appropriate person, but don't rehash it. *Let it go!*

You can also start being aware and responding to double binds. Take a stand and express yourself. One way to begin to address double binds and stereotypes is to become media literate. The goal of media literacy is to provide consumers with knowledge, education, and critical thinking skills and strategies to analyze and evaluate what they're exposed to.

Ask yourself if you're consuming valid, honorable representations of women. Are the images demonstrating behaviors you want to imitate, or you want your daughter to emulate? People who are repeatedly exposed to hurtful behaviors (through media or otherwise) become desensitized to them and become the adults who behave in hurtful ways to others. Take authority over your media environment—for yourself and your children.

If you're a mother, aunt, neighbor, or friend, or you have a female you mentor, help her be more cognizant and educated about the messages, stereotypes, double binds, and media influences she receives. Help her critically question what she's consuming by talking to her about its impact—what does she think about the way women are portrayed?

Bring awareness to the issue (as early as possible) and help her sort through and question the stereotypes and messages she receives as truth. Encourage her, support her, and remind her that she has the choice in how to act; she's in control of the woman she wants to be—and so are you.

I know I drilled down deep into the whole "women don't support each other" topic, and a few people may get upset with me. That's okay. It's easier to focus on how men unjustly kept us from obtaining leadership roles but that won't work for two reasons. First, we can't do anything other than educate them to change their behavior, which may or may not work. But, ladies, remember, they aren't the one's screaming from the rooftops for more promotions and equal pay.

Second, we have to demonstrate that, as a whole, we're

worthy of leadership positions. It's ultimately up to us. When we behave in ways that are blatantly hateful, and downright cannibalistic, I don't blame them for not wanting us on their teams! Hell, who would want to be on a team like that anyway? I know I wouldn't!

We can no longer pretend women support each other all the time and that men are the reason we're not advancing in our careers. We have to look at the reality and the bigger picture. Unfortunately, we're dealing with problems in both camps. However, there is hope. With the current focus on beneficial traits necessary for strong leadership and how women tend to lead with a more transformational approach than men, I think the tides may be turning in our favor. Now we have to get out of our own way and act as the leaders we're meant to be.

PART FOUR
Looking in the Mirror

We've discussed three of the four challenges women reported battling on their way to the upper ranks of corporate America. So, in a quick review: (1) women are challenged with balancing family and career, (2) they're currently challenged because of limited advancement opportunities in their organization or as a perceived result of their age, and (3) they experience a lack of support from both male and female colleagues in their attempt to conquer the corner suite. What on earth could possibly be the last challenge women shared in their common experiences?

Sadly, it's ourselves. More than half the women shared how they lacked confidence in themselves and their abilities, regardless of their position and accomplishments. In chapter 3 we talked about how the lack of self-confidence can manifest itself in relationships with others, with insecurity as the key driver behind the mean girl epidemic. But let's take a deeper look into how dealing with our own fear, insecurities, and low self-confidence can affect ourselves and the world around us. Let's tackle confidence.

Confidence Defined

What is confidence, exactly? How do you define it? Is it a feeling? Is it a belief? A thought? An attitude? A concoction of all the above? According to the almighty *Webster's Dictionary*, *confidence* is a noun; by definition it means: "the act of confiding, trusting, or putting faith in; trust; reliance; belief in; that in which faith is put or reliance had; the state of mind characterized by one's reliance on himself, or his circumstances; a feeling of self-sufficiency; such assurance as leads to a feeling of security; self-reliance."

Confidence is having full trust in something, or a belief in the powers, trustworthiness, or reliability of a person or thing. Self-confidence, then, means a belief in oneself and one's powers or abilities. Self-confidence. Self-reliance. Assurance. In their book *The Confidence Code*, Katty Kay and Claire Shipman state: "We were at last confident about the way we wanted to define confidence. We felt all the more so when one of our most stalwart guides through this tricky terrain, Richard Petty, a psychology professor at Ohio State University, who has spent decades focused on the subject, managed to put all we had learned into appealingly clear terms: Confidence is the stuff that turns thoughts into action" (Kay & Shipman, 2014, p. 50).

By that definition, confidence is the catalyst that turns one's thoughts into actions. I agree with that, for the most part, but I'd like to challenge you because I think it goes even deeper.

Never mistake motion for action."

~ ERNEST HEMINGWAY

How do you gain confidence? Is it merely taking action? I mean, don't we all take action? Even hamsters on a wheel are in motion. But, I believe confidence is found when you commit to living in a space that's beyond simply taking action. Confidence is developed when you keep moving forward, making decisions in alignment with your values, even in the face of adversity.

It's what you gain when you wake up every day, amidst life's biggest challenges, and keep going, with your shoulders back and your head high. Confidence is what you grow when you've faced adversity head on and didn't crumble—because you knew your purpose and adhered to your integrity. It's what you realize you have when you look back on some of the hardest parts of life and say to yourself, "Damn! I don't know how I handled that, but I came out on the other side—I stayed true to what I know and grew stronger in spite of that."

I believe we find our confidence at the intersection of courage and faith. Confidence is gained when you have the courage to step out and grow, after failure, stagnation, or loss, and not collapse in hardship's grip. Confidence is what you find when you have the courage to wake up every day amidst the dark circumstances of life and keep moving forward, when all you really want to do is stay in bed with the covers pulled over your head. Confidence is found when you can look back at what you've accomplished and gain strength from your previous achievements; your past gains give you the courage to move forward, even in uncertain circumstances.

However, I don't believe confidence is found in courage alone; it requires faith to thrive. Faith to believe in yourself, to know your significance, your gifts and abilities, and to continue to press forward despite difficult circumstances. Faith is required to find your confidence, by taking an honest look at your values, gifts, and talents in life to see what makes you special—what makes you uniquely you.

Confidence is found in resilience, which is developed through perseverance. Confidence is found in the faith of knowing full well you have a unique purpose and importance that goes beyond any title or accomplishment. Confidence is found in realizing your significance. So, with that definition and through that lens, let's talk about the problem. Why do so many women lack confidence?

CHAPTER 17

The Battle Within

I always did something I was a little not ready to do. I think that's how you grow. When there's that moment of "Wow, I'm not really sure I can do this," and you push through those moments, that's when you have a breakthrough.

~ MARISSA MAYER

Women, we face a battle from within. Actually, the lack of confidence isn't something specific to women, but that's the focus I'll maintain here, as research shows self-doubt is more common for females. Internal barriers can alter a woman's behavior and hold us back from achieving and accomplishing our goals. Because of fear, we consistently underestimate ourselves and our capabilities.

Fear is the root cause of a vast number of challenges women face: fear of saying the wrong thing; fear of not being liked; fear of failure; fear of success; fear of rejection; fear of not being able to handle it all; fear of fear—the list goes on. Fear is what we use as our excuse to play small.

Studies have affirmed that women outnumber men in obtaining graduate degrees, and we hold more than half of all professional-level jobs in the U.S. workforce. However, according to the Center for American Progress, we haven't moved into positions of power and prominence at near the rate we should have, based on our representation and successes in higher education, and the entry- and mid-level workforce. Hell, according to a 2015 *New York Times* article, there are more CEOs named John than there are women CEOs!

The reason we're not advancing isn't because we're not educated enough, or there aren't enough women in the workforce to move into roles of authority. We clearly see we're positioning ourselves to take the lead in business by getting the degrees and moving into management. Our problem, though, is because of fear we play it safe. Women, as a whole, have a fundamental lack of belief in our own abilities, value, and worth, which impedes our ambition and holds us back.

One participant, Fran, relayed how her lack of confidence was evidenced in how she spoke: "To this day, when you're the only female in the room, you find yourself apologizing or speaking with qualifiers, by saying, 'I don't know if this is right, but…' When we do start speaking we have to qualify everything instead of just saying, 'Hey! I have an idea!' And I find myself doing that."

How many of us speak in qualifiers? We set ourselves up to not be taken seriously when we preface our thoughts with disqualifying phrases. When speaking with qualifiers, we negate the credibility of our suggestion or idea. And if you don't believe in your own thoughts and ideas, who else will?

Another participant, a hospital CFO, relayed, "A lot of my problem was my own lack of confidence, of being the only female in a predominantly male room. In meetings I would find myself writing notes to my male friends telling them my ideas instead of just speaking up on my own. I had a hard time speaking up with my own voice. Finally one of my male colleagues said, 'I'm not your voice. You have to be. You're a VP in this company and if you don't find it now, you never will.'

"So he pushed me out of that. And when I started speaking

out, I realized, 'Hey, my opinions aren't stupid!' Or, even if they were, it wasn't the end of the world. And I've realized, I don't know if it was maturity or, 'Oh my god, I'm a CFO,' but I've realized I made it here for a reason and my opinions do count."

According to a global, eight-year study of more than 985,000 people, published in the *Journal of Personality and Social Psychology*, the disparity in self-belief between women and men is not specific to American women, it's universal (Bleidorn et al., 2016). "In nearly all cultures, men have higher self-esteem. But the difference lies in the *magnitude* of the gap."

Surprisingly, the gap is more pronounced—greater—in industrialized Western countries than it is in developing countries. As such, the disparity between how highly men think of themselves as opposed to how little women think of themselves is greatest in more developed countries, which are the ones we'd expect to be the least.

Why is that? Could it be that for centuries females have been socialized to be silent, play nice, play by the rules, and take care of others (sometimes at our own expense)? I don't see how this *wouldn't* affect our confidence and sense of worth and value. At the core, we've been told by society we're of lesser significance since before we were born. And, could the gap be more expansive in Western cultures because of how we, as a society, have such a high demand, especially on females, for perfection—we must have the perfect house, perfectly behaved children, husband, clothes, hair, makeup, job, car, life?

Think of print, media, commercials, billboards, magazines, and all the advertising targeting women, which are constantly feeding us lies that we aren't "enough." That is, until we buy the right shoes, bras, or devices that nip and tuck us to the point where we can't even breathe! The basic responsibility of advertising is to make us feel so dissatisfied that we feel compelled to fix ourselves with their stuff, whether we need it or not.

Because we believe we aren't enough, we're relentlessly confronted with the message to compare our "have-nots" to those that have. The incredible part is, amazingly, if we buy whatever their product is, they can fix us! (Sarcasm intended.) Whatever they're doing is working, too, as women drive 70-80 percent of all consumer purchasing. Generally, we're all guilty of buying into our lack—myself included.

Recently I was shopping for an under-the-formal-dress "device" to wear to ensure my love handles wouldn't show when I went to an awards show. I was at the department store perusing the plethora of choices and came across a full-body suit that was, no kidding, made from the same material as a scuba suit. I kept touching it and couldn't help but laugh at how obnoxious, rubbery, and slimy it felt.

People were looking at me weirdly (I mean, I guess a lady by herself cracking up in the lingerie department does look rather suspicious), but I was just amazed at the lengths we think we need to go in the name of beauty. It's so sad to me, but entire industries are making a killing off our insecurities and lack of confidence.

Now, understand me when I say, it's not the beauty industry, or men, or our bosses, or history, or whatever else we may blame that's the enemy. I'm also not saying it's a cardinal sin to wear makeup (believe me, I'm from the South, where you don't leave the house without your lip gloss), have nice clothes, feel pretty, or even wear a scuba suit if that's what suits your fancy. But the problem lies when we believe we have to have these things or other's approval to be a better, more fulfilled, whole, complete, significant, valued, confident person.

Ladies, we have to get back to the root, and the most threatening enemy to women is women. It's the way we allow other women to treat each other, it's the way we treat ourselves, and worst—the fact that we give ourselves permission to opt out of taking on new, albeit sometimes uncomfortable, tasks.

Given that success, and ultimately confidence, only comes as a result of branching out and taking risks—and women are less willing to take risks especially when it comes to their careers—over time they end up missing out on opportunities that could potentially advance their career. One participant, Jane, a hospital CEO, said, "My greatest challenge was overcoming the perception of just being a chief nursing officer. I was doing so much and I got pigeonholed into that line of thinking. It was hard to see me as more than the vision I'd created. I wanted more, but didn't feel like I'd be considered skilled enough for anything more than what I was doing. There's something called the imposter syndrome. And as women leaders one of the things we typically deal with, we deal with this feeling of 'I'm a fake. I don't really have the talent necessary for the position I find myself in, and it's just a mistake I'm here.' So now and then that little sort of doubt creeps in."

Jane wasn't the only woman who talked about that little voice telling her she's not qualified to be in a position of power she'd worked hard for. The Imposter Syndrome, a term coined in 1978 by two American psychologists Pauline Clance and Suzanne Imes, is described as a feeling of phoniness in those who believe they aren't creative, capable, or intelligent, despite having solid evidence of high achievements. These high achievers have a solid fear of being "found out" or that someone will expose them for being a fraud.

A colleague of mine shared the moment she realized she had to put her big-girl pants on and exercise the confidence she seldom thought she had. She was hired as a contractor for a well-known author/speaker/coach as his Director of Content. Even though she'd already survived a slew of interviews with seven people, from subordinates and colleagues to the COO and CEO, she couldn't be offered a full-time employment position until she met with the latter face-to-face.

Because this was such a high-level position, one that would directly collaborate with him in person, he had to personally extend the offer after spending time with her. After a month of working through scheduling, the day came to drive two hours to his home to spend a time in a brainstorming meeting with him and one of his business partners. She was ready to meet him, had researched the position enough to know she could handle the work, and felt confident in her abilities.

However, that confidence quickly ran dry. She recounted, "When I walked into his home and heard his voice on a phone call on the other side of the wall, my mouth became dry and my stomach ached. I'd only ever heard him on television and watched videos of him on stage. I thought, 'This is really happening' and then I thought, 'What am I doing here? I don't belong here. I'm a fraud!' But, in the few minutes it took for him to finish his phone call, I changed my thoughts to, 'He's just a man. He's just a man. I have experience. I am smart. I have a good sense of humor that can work in any situation. I've got this. He's just a man.'"

When he finally walked into the room, she saw his grin was as big in person as it is in the media. His first words were, "It's great to finally meet you. I've heard great things about you." The next ten hours were spent brainstorming ideas in his living room and before she left, he said, "Welcome to the team." It was because of this experience that she eventually chose to go back to a contractor status, where she could work with him without managing a team and take on additional clients, without a conflict. Within the year she launched her own company and has never looked back.

But how many women allow that voice of fear to reign over their actions? How much power do we give to that voice that keeps us from applying for that position, tackling that new challenge, asking for that raise, stepping out and starting that company we dream of, or negotiating the higher salary? I believe the power we allow that voice to have is part of what keeps us from advancing.

Although several organizations have made committed efforts to attract, retain, and promote female talent, no clear evidence exists of the best ways to tackle the shortage. According to the 2014-2015 Global Leadership Forecast, nearly three-fourths of company high-potential programs aren't working (Development Dimensions International, Inc., 2015). However, businesses can take all the action they want to increase the number of females in leadership and improve leadership capacity for women all day long, but their actions alone won't make up for the shortage of women leaders. One of the reasons, though, is due to the lack of confidence women reported experiencing.

Research has shown women aren't applying for positions of advancement at the same rate as men. As previously referenced, women will only apply for positions when they meet 100 percent of the role qualifications, whereas men will apply when they meet 60 percent of the qualifications.

Another participant, Kerry, confirmed this when she explained how she almost allowed her lack of confidence to keep her from her current role, saying, "I knew the position was open and it was the role I really wanted. I waited until the last few days to throw my name in for consideration because I didn't think I'd get the job. I just kept thinking to myself, 'There's tons of people here, there's no way I'm going to get this job.' But I did." But—she did; she raised her hand and got the job.

Having confidence is crucial for so many aspects of our life, and I don't think our employment is the only area affected by our self-doubt. One participant, Liz, a healthcare CEO, said, "Do I feel like I struggle with confidence? At home I do, because I'm not there as much and I don't know as much. If my kids struggle in school I feel like it's because I'm not there to help as much as I should be. And, I know, being in my position here at work, I feel like I struggle with confidence. I have things I wanted to be doing in the company and we aren't doing them. And it's my lack of confidence of not knowing how to put it all together. And I'm afraid that I can't keep it all together—at work or at home."

In the working world, however, career advancement, promotion, income, and salary increases all depend on our ability to show up feeling confident and secure in who we are. Interestingly, confidence was one of the only significant differences found between women and men leaders in the study previously referenced, with leadership effectiveness and abilities reportedly being equal.

The gap in confidence between women and men starts in the early stages of their careers, but closes near mid-level career; then the gap enlarges at high levels. Females in top organizational ranks aren't nearly as confident as males, and it's not a generational difference either.

The biggest issue holding women back is the power we give to fear. Ultimately, what holds us back is *us*. We wait for the approval of others, our feelings to change, or *things* to magically make us more confident, but the answer lies in ourselves—at the intersection of courage and faith. My friend Carol said, "I led a teleconference on January 2nd with hundreds of women. And on January 11th I'd already gotten reports from women saying they are letting the self-talk win. I got an email from one woman at 3:00 a.m. today, and she said she's starting her own business, but she already doesn't feel hopeful. Her skill set is not there, she thought she'd be further ahead. On January 1st she made the decision to succeed, and here we were ten days later and she's already buying into the negative self-talk."

Confidence is found when you have the courage to be resilient, when you learn to persevere, and not allow your success, *however you define it,* to be optional. But that's just half the equation; faith is the other factor. Confidence is found by determining our values, and the realization of knowing we're here for a deeper purpose. Our confidence is realized when we identify our significance—not through material things or in others' eyes but through our own eyes.

CHAPTER 18

Identifying What Defines You

Don't be intimidated by what you don't know.
That can be your greatest strength and ensure
that you do things differently from everyone else.

~ SARA BLAKELY

Have you ever heard the saying, "People don't plan to fail; they fail to plan"? Values are very similar to plans—Peter Marshall said it best: "If you don't stand for something, you'll fall for anything." When you don't know what your values are and what you stand for, you may find yourself so far away from being the person you intended to be that you look up and wonder how you got there.

I'm directionally challenged and it's a running joke in my family. I've actually gotten lost going the right way on a one-way street (it was in high school, got home at 4:00 am, not a pretty ending, but that's another story). Although I grew up in the Dallas area and have lived in the vicinity nearly all my life, I still put destinations in my GPS—even if I've been to the location several times. It's my way to verify that I'm on the right path, that I've not gotten lost, and it reassures me I'll be arriving where I'm supposed to and at the specified time.

This past Christmas I was driving with my son to my parents' home and I didn't put their address in my phone's GPS.

My dad and stepmom have lived in the same house for more than 15 years, but it's out in the country about an hour and a half from my house. I thought I'd recall how to get there from memory, but unfortunately I got lost. Despite my better judgment and the knowledge of the fact that I can get lost in a paper bag, I winged it. I hadn't meant to get lost, but I did. I'd attempted to pursue my goal by instinct and surroundings and didn't rely on the habit that serves me well.

How many of us pursue goals, or even life, that way? We go after the next shiny new object and make decisions that potentially violate our health, happiness, and overall well-being. Or we say we're committed to one thing but act in a way that doesn't support our words, or even our foundational values. What hangs in the balance is our integrity.

Self-awareness and reflection are unique elements of the human condition; they're truly a gift. When your values are not in alignment with your choices, thoughts, words, and actions, incongruity permeates all aspects of your life. Your core values are the center of who you are, as they're the guiding principles that help you make rational decisions. They're representative of what's most important to each of us.

Knowing your core values and being courageous enough to act on them, even when it's hard, is the foundation for integrity. But there's more to the equation than core values—it's imperative that you not only know what you stand for but also identify your non-negotiables.

I was recently talking to a friend of mine, Carol, who I mentioned previously. She's in the commercial real estate industry. She's been incredibly successful and I asked her where she found her confidence to compete in an industry that's predominantly male. She responded, "I found my confidence in the necessity to have it—in the necessity and as a necessity. I knew I wasn't going to be successful in real estate without it and I started asking myself, 'What are you afraid of'? And I still struggle with having the negative self-talk sometimes. We all do; but when I hear it I don't just automatically believe it, and buy into it. I ask myself, 'Where is the evidence to support that thought?' I'm an immigrant, and my parents are immigrants. How many black immigrant women do you know in this industry? I have to constantly remember that my confidence is out of necessity. It's not optional."

Carol's confidence in herself is one of her core values and a direct correlation to her success; it's her non-negotiable. Being confident in herself has been a guiding principle that governs her thoughts, decisions, and actions. She's been able to make an incredible career out of a male-dominated industry when she started her journey with no money, no experience, and no network. All because she didn't give herself a choice of whether or not to believe in herself. The option-out clause, a term used in real estate, was not on the table.

Another friend, Pam, relayed, "So many women don't live into their confidence because they don't know what's non-negotiable for them. I know my values, and that's one thing, but some women have not clearly identified what they are not willing to negotiate on. When you wake up five years later and you don't know who you are or how you got there because you were too afraid to say no, or 'You're not allowed to talk to me like that,' or 'No, I will not pass this flawed budget,' or whatever the scenario may be. Those are beyond values. The value structure is made of those things that are important—great. But when you're backed up against the wall and your source of income is threatened because you worked 12 years to get to that position, the confidence tripod begins to fail. Values change but you have to define your non-negotiables. Meaning, I am willing to go to the valley but still keep my confidence in tact because I am not willing to do these certain things."

Core values are like fingerprints—everyone has them and they're what make us unique. Your values are what guide your decisions, what define you, and what govern your judgment. Values aren't one-size-fits-all. What's right, or even acceptable, for one doesn't automatically equate to being right for all. They'll probably morph a little over time, but foundationally they'll stay the same. There are typically five to seven values, or traits, that when clear to us, give us a deeper sense of who we are and how we adjust to the world. They're what defines us.

Many people, when they aren't in touch with their core values and non-negotiables, simply get carried along through life by the influence of their surroundings. Everywhere we turn, we're constantly under a barrage of noise of who we are, who we should be, what we should buy, what we should do, or what we need to make us happy.

The bombardment of messages about what's important and what makes us valuable—from family, friends, peers, culture, advertisers, life experiences, the voices in our head—doesn't stop. Some have good intentions and others have their wallets open. Being in touch with your core values is imperative to being in charge of your own life.

When I attended orientation at Pepperdine University for graduate school, we spent a weekend getting to know our cohort members, which was crucial since we'd be spending the next four years with them. However, more importantly, we completed a self-reflection exercise, which was, for me, life-changing. We had to write our 80th birthday toast. We had to consider who we were committed to being and acting. What was the person we wanted to be remembered for?

While completing that exercise, I broke down in tears. It occurred to me I wasn't living as the person I wanted to be remembered for; I feared that if I died right then I'd be known for being too busy: too busy to be with friends, too busy to listen to my children, too busy to prioritize time to go on dates with my husband. And I feared I'd be remembered for being too demanding—expecting others to live up to unrealistic expectations that could never be met.

As a result of that exercise, I decided it was time to make a change. I wanted to live life as the person for which I wanted to be remembered. I got a notecard and wrote down four words (that have become my values) on a notecard: faith-full, connected, inspiring, intentional. I put that notecard on my bathroom mirror, and every day when I'm getting ready and putting on my makeup I see those words. I look at myself in the mirror and ask, "Who do you want to be today? How are you going to show up? Who are you going to connect with? Who are you going to inspire?"

And, honestly, it's not always easy to be "on" every day, but I do the best I can. I'm now more conscious of the legacy I'm leaving behind, because I'm aware I'm creating that eighty-year-old person every single day—in every thought, decision, word, and action. And so are you.

Identifying what matters to you, whether that's honesty, connectedness, career success, giving of yourself—it could be anything—gives you a blueprint for life continuity. Values serve as your life roadmap, or compass, to keep you on track. And they can't be just an off-the-cuff commitment, or one that's given lip service either. Something defines you, whether it's the values you want them to be or not. What are yours?

Whether you know your values or not, I want you to do some thinking and self-reflection. When you have some alone time and a quiet place to think, I want you to answer the following (and remember there are no right or wrong answers):

Right now:

- The values, traits, or characteristics that define me are _____.

- My identity is found in _____.

- My non-negotiables are _____.

- I allow _____ to be optional.
- I find my value in _____.

Ideally:

- The values, traits, or characteristics
  I want to define me are _____.
- My identity is found in _____.
- My non-negotiables are _____.
- I allow _____ to be optional.
- I'd find my value in _____.

CHAPTER 19

Developing Resilience

"It is our choices... that show what we truly are, far more than our abilities."

~ J. K ROWLING, *HARRY POTTER AND THE CHAMBER OF SECRETS*

In 1999 Janie, a thirty-seven-year old completely able-bodied woman, was shopping alone at her local grocery store. She picked up a 12-pack of diet soda from a seven-foot-tall display and the entire product display, which had been built just seven hours earlier, came tumbling down on top of her head. She woke up in the hospital with no recollection of what had happened or where she was. All she could remember was that she had a four-year-old son and wanted to know where he was.

Janie spent two years in and out of the hospital, having multiple surgeries, including the addition of titanium rods in her neck. She had severe memory loss, chronic headaches, and seizures, which prevented her from driving. With years of daily therapy, she had to relearn how to walk (without vomiting), talk, read, and write. She had to learn how to function again—and how to live.

Janie was engaged at the time of the accident to a man she'd been in a relationship with for nearly nine years. Due to the location of her rehabilitation center being an hour away from the home shared with her fiancé, she moved in with her sister, who drove her to her daily therapy appointments. However, the calls from her fiancé slowly dissipated. At one point, Janie's sister drove her to check on him and the home, only to find out he was gone. He'd left.

The house was empty and hadn't been maintained for an unknown amount of time; none of the bills had been paid. As a result, Janie lost her home and was in financial ruins. To complicate matters, neither the grocery store chain nor the soda company would claim responsibility for the accident. Her lawsuit against both was dismissed on grounds of frivolity.

Today, nearly 18 years after the accident, Janie has rebuilt her life. She leaned on her mother and four sisters to help get her through the roughest years of her life. She attributes her successful healing to the support she had from her family and the tough love her mom showed her a few years following the incident. Janie recalls, "My mom came to the hospital one day and said, 'Look, I can't come to the hospital anymore. I'm not going to visit you or be around you anymore until you get yourself together. You need to decide—are you going to be here and be pitiful or are you going to be grateful you're alive and figure this out? It hurts me too much to see you like this. You have to get it together.' That was the conversation that really turned me around."

In spite of the accident, Janie has worked diligently on her recovery and is now Chief Operating Officer of a large medical clinic with 200 employees that serves 25,000 patients a year. Her goal in life, she says, is to make a better life for others.

How do some people suffer devastating hardships and rebound? How do people stumble, fall, and get back up again only to climb to greater success? We all have trials and tribulations. Some are more overwhelming than others, but none of us are immune to the highs and lows life brings.

What is resilience exactly? According to the American Psychological Association, resilience is the process of adapting well in the face of adversity, trauma, tragedy, threats, or significant sources of stress—such as family and relationship problems, serious health problems, or workplace and financial stressors (American Psychological Association, n.d.).

Resilience is being able to persevere, and bounce back when difficult experiences, circumstances, or events occur. Years of research confirm that our contentment with life isn't dependent on how many times we experience sadness, worries, or regrets, or even the intensity of these events. Instead, however, our life satisfaction is determined by how we deal with the experiences we go through.

Although once thought to be a trait-like characteristic you're either born with or you're not, recent research has determined resilience is also a skill that can be taught—some people are born more resilient than others, but evidence shows it can also be learned over time. Therefore, resilience has been defined as "the developable capacity to rebound or bounce back from adversity, conflict, failure, or even positive events, progress, and increased responsibility" (Luthans, 2002, p. 702).

Resilience is as critical in business, if not more than, integrity, intelligence, ambition, or analytic ability. Resilience is what helps employees bounce back from layoffs, setbacks, organizational change, ambiguity, and uncertainty. Dean Becker, the President and CEO of Adaptive Learning Systems, a company that develops and delivers programs and training for resilience, said a person's level of resilience is more important than education, training, or experience, as one's resilience will determine if he or she is capable of succeeding. Becker says, "That's true in the cancer ward, it's true in the Olympics, and it's true in the boardroom" (Coutu, 2002). But why do some people fold easily whereas others persevere in difficult circumstances? What is "it" about resilience that gets some people through life and makes them stronger than before they faced adversity?

Components of Resiliency

Much research and talk in the past few decades has focused on the power of positive thinking, but is that what resilience is? Can you put your positive thinking hat on and hopefully believe your way into resilience, and therefore, confidence? Not entirely. Resilience does require a certain level of optimism, but only as long as it doesn't alter your perception of reality.

Although there are several theories of what resilience is, most of them encompass three key components. The first component is that resilient people have a strong, realistic acceptance of circumstances. Second, resilient people hold deeply to values that life has meaning and purpose. Lastly, resilient people have remarkable skill and ability to improvise. And, the good news is, resilience can be learned by anyone through behaviors, actions, and mind-set. So let's look at each component of resiliency.

Reality: Take Off Your Rose-Colored Glasses

The first component of resilience is that one must have a solid, sound understanding of reality. Resilience is more than positive thinking; you can't think only happy thoughts when dealing with a difficult reality, especially since most people fall into denial's fateful grip. A firm grasp of circumstances is needed and only thinking optimistically misses the mark; I believe it's basically the equivalent to sticking your head in the sand during a windstorm—not a lot of good that'll do!

The company I founded, KidsCare Therapy, opened for

business on October 27, 2003. Two days later, on October 29, we were sued. Although the case was more than likely going to be unsubstantiated, we had no money in the bank to fight it. I'm not a quitter, but I felt like there was no way out. I would have optioned out at that point, and very much wanted to, but I was putting payroll on my credit cards and couldn't afford to quit.

My husband worked the night shift at a warehouse and he'd come home in the morning, long after I should have been up and moving, and some days I'd be in bed under the covers. He'd look at me and say, "Get up! If it was easy, everyone would do it." And he was right. It wasn't easy, but quitting wasn't optional.

Thankfully the attorney's office we'd worked with to establish the company was willing to allow us to make payments, but the future looked bleak. I'll never forget going into the lawyer's office to prepare for trial and she told us everything that could happen—the highs, lows, good, bad, ugly, and very real possibilities. It was scary to know the odds, but I was grateful to know what we were up against and to not be promised sunshine and roses. As much as we hated the circumstances, we were ready to face the case.

In the end, we settled the suit, but through thoughtful preparation we'd established a contingency plan. Thankfully we didn't have to act on it, because we'd have been living on loans and lines of credit for a very long time. But the point in all of it is this: when you look reality square in the eyes, you allow yourself to prepare, to run the race, to endure, and to survive.

Meaning and Purpose

The second component to resilience is being able to see a situation's meaning and purpose through the circumstances, which is directly linked to seeing reality for what it is. Seeing the silver lining behind why something has happened or using a horrible situation to help others is a gift. Resilient people create constructs regarding their hardships to devise meaning for themselves and others.

When tragedy strikes, most people ask themselves, "Why me?" To build resilience, turn the question around and ask, "Why not me?" or "What, through this time, will I gain that I wouldn't have had otherwise?" Most researchers agree, the way resilient people are able to transition from current hardships to a better, more fulfilled future is through creating meaning from the painful lesson. Know that trials and tribulations are the only way to persevere; and perseverance builds character; and character builds hope. And truly, what do you have left if you don't have hope?

Viktor Frankl, a psychiatrist who survived a Nazi death camp and authored *Man's Search for Meaning*, summed it up best by saying, "We must never forget that we may also find meaning in life even when confronted with a hopeless situation, when facing a fate that cannot be changed."

Creativity Opens Opportunity

The third component to building resiliency amidst turbulence is learning to think creatively with the situation at hand by making the most of what you have. Resilient people, and companies, tend to see opportunity when others see roadblocks, relying on improvisation as a core skill. Being able to easily adapt to change by bending and flowing with the tides is a necessity.

A commitment to building your resiliency reserves is imperative to thrive and grow in difficult circumstances. During turbulent times, focus on what you have the power to control. As Albert Einstein said, "Out of clutter, find simplicity. From discord, find harmony. In the middle of difficulty lies opportunity."

Even though the situation may be out of your control, you do have the power to determine how you'll react to it, and that's actually where the control lies. To help reconcile our meaning and place in the world, Frankl believed that "between stimulus and response there is a space. In that space is our power to choose our response. In our response lies our growth and freedom."

Having greater control over your thoughts and emotions is the key to greater resilience and confidence.

One way to take back control over your old self-defeating thoughts, behaviors, and emotions is through emotional agility, a process described by Dr. Susan David, a psychologist and faculty member at Harvard Medical School. Emotional agility, as described by David in her book by the same name, is not a system to ensure you think more positively or just control your thoughts; rather, it's when you allow flexibility with your feelings and thoughts so you can potentially react more optimally to daily circumstances. She attributes emotional agility to the key to well-being and success. I believe having greater control over your thoughts and emotions is the key to greater resilience and confidence.

Emotional agility is comprised of four practices adapted from Acceptance and Commitment Therapy (ACT):

1. **Recognize the patterns that keep you hooked.** Identifying that your self-defeating thoughts, behaviors, and emotions are keeping you stuck is the critical first

step to change. Our inner critic is typically not indifferent or unbiased, and recognizing your patterns gives you the chance to ask yourself who's in control: the thought or the thinker?

2. **Identify and label the thoughts and emotions you experience.** Labeling your thoughts as thoughts and emotions as emotions allows you the ability to decide if they're helpful or hurtful to you.

3. **Accept your thoughts and emotions by showing up.** Being open to your ideas and emotions helps you pay attention and allows you the time to experience them. Acceptance is a requirement for change and you can't change your circumstances, or yourself, until you show up.

4. **Commit to upholding your values.** We've already discussed the importance of knowing and living by your values. Being committed to what makes you "you," and what matters most to you is what life should be about. When you know and adhere to your values, you're able to move forward with confidence, rather than being led by others or striving to pretend.

CHAPTER 20

Path to Purpose

I believe we're all put on this planet for a purpose, and we all have a different purpose... When you connect with that love and that compassion, that's when everything unfolds.

~ ELLEN DEGENERES

In 2005 I had a pulmonary embolism (PE), which is a blood clot in the lungs. I spent more than a week recovering in the hospital. In the U.S. nearly a million cases of PEs are reported every year. They are dangerous, with a fatality rate of approximately 30 percent. Out of that 30 percent, about one in four dies suddenly. I was lucky to be alive.

While recovering, the thought occurred to me that I was now living life on 70 percent. My simple math was this: we're born at 100 percent capacity, and I was one of the "lucky" to survive after experiencing a PE. Since 30 percent of those with PEs die, and I remained, I was now living life on 70 percent (100 percent - 30 percent = 70 percent). Makes perfect sense!

I'm a perfectionist and strive to have all As. I wasn't thrilled with the fact that I was just barely passing, but I was alive, so I thought, "Hey, I guess I'll take it." I carried on with life, had my third child, and went about my business living life on 70 percent.

Another Challenge along the Way

Fast-forward to September 2012. I was recovering from having recently undergone gum grafting, a minor dental procedure, and just didn't feel right. The week after the surgery, I had difficulty with activities of daily living and stayed in bed the majority of the time. On Sunday I called the oral surgeon, explained how I was feeling, and was told to stop taking the steroids he'd prescribed. I did as instructed and began to feel better.

The next day, Monday, I felt a little better—not great, but better. I resumed my school studies, as I'd begun my doctoral journey the month prior. On Tuesday, September 18, 2012, I woke up to get ready for the day. I went to the kitchen sink to wash my hair (it's weird, I know, but stay with me). I turned on the water, and watched it run from the faucet. I looked from the water, to the shampoo, to the conditioner, and back again.

I didn't know what to do next. I repeated the process, and still had no clue of how to proceed. I turned off the water and turned it back on again, thinking it would spark some semblance of an idea of what to do. Nothing. I waited a minute, knowing fully that I needed to wash my hair but couldn't remember how.

My husband was home and I told him what I was experiencing. He already thinks I'm a hypochondriac, so I was hesitant to tell him, but I did. He encouraged me to lie back down, thinking I needed to rest, so I did. My next-door neighbor, Lindsay, who happens to be one of my best friends, called to check on me and when I told her what happened, she urged me to go to the doctor. I didn't want to make a big deal about it, so I refused, saying I'd be fine if I just got more rest. She said she'd come by after running errands to check on me.

What seemed like hours went by and then the doorbell rang. I knew it was Lindsay coming to see me, and the last thing I remember was my husband getting up to answer the door.

I woke up in the hospital a day later to my husband standing over me telling me I'd had a stroke. I was thirty-seven years old. On Thursday, the next day, I underwent a seven-hour brain surgery to inject medication to bust the clot. During the procedure, the doctors actually found two clots. I'd had a cerebral venous sinus thrombosis, a rare stroke affecting about five in one million people each year.

After surgery I stayed in ICU and once transitioned to a step-down unit, I began testing to see if I needed speech, physical, or occupational therapy services. Ironically, the only one I qualified for was speech therapy, due to my memory loss and word-finding difficulties.

I was projected to be in ICU for ten days. However, instead, I went home on the tenth day, on September 28, 2012—the day before my thirty-eighth birthday. The neurologist later told my husband and me that 50 percent of the people who have the same type of stroke don't even make it to the hospital; I was lucky to be alive. I'm now living life on 20 percent (70 percent – 50 percent = 20 percent). My son says statistics don't work that way, but they do in my logic.

Instead of being disappointed or looking at my odds like I was failing (20 percent is definitely not a passing grade where I come from), I started to see life from a different perspective. I realized how precious our time here is and how none of us are promised our ideal concept of growing old gracefully. I'm committed to living life on my 20 percent and showing others they can do the same—on whatever percent they have!

What to Know about Purpose

Mark Twain said, "The two most important days of your life are the day you were born and the day you find out why." You don't have to have a health scare or a near-death experience to come to the realization that you may, in fact, have a deeper meaning to serve in life than you currently are. Do you connect with any of the following words (read them slowly and take time to really consider): Fast-paced? Office? Crazy? Family? Busy? Disconnected? Meetings? 24/7? Chaotic? Harried? Nonstop? Friends? Turbulent? Social Media? Loud? Stressed? Hectic? Exhausted? Drained? Depleted?

The world we live in is increasingly demanding and it's getting more and more difficult to hear above the noise. In Dr. Brene Brown's TEDx Houston talk, she reported, "We are the most in debt, obese, addicted, and medicated cohort in U.S. history." We medicate, shop, eat, drink, and numb away the thoughts and chaos, and then sleep, wake up, rinse, and repeat.

Have you seen the documentary *I Am,* by Tom Shadyak, the director behind such Hollywood hits as *Ace Ventura: Pet Detective; Liar, Liar; Bruce Almighty;* and *The Nutty Professor*? Without revealing too many of the details, Shadyak has a revelation and begins to question what's wrong with our world, and he's curious about what we can do to make it right. It's an 80-minute documentary I highly recommend that discusses the ills of society not being what we think—war, hate, poverty, crime, environmental crisis, or even greed. Instead, he discovered those are merely symptoms of a bigger problem. Through his research and discussions with scientists, psychologists, artists, environmentalists, authors, activists, philosophers, entrepreneurs, and others, he finds a much bigger purpose.

It's more important than ever for us to pause, take a deep breath, and connect to our deeper purpose and meaning we have in life. The single most important thing we carry with us in life, whether at work, home, or anywhere else, is *who we are at our core*—not what we can do, our title, or our accomplishments. Our confidence is found when we know we have a purpose and we live connected to that purpose.

When you're connected to your purpose, you feel a strong, peaceful light glowing from within; it comes with an absolute "yes" and not questionable uncertainty. You may not be able to describe it, but you will feel it. Here's what I know about purpose:

1. **Only you can identify and define your purpose.** Your friends, family, peers, colleagues, or anyone with an opinion will be able to tell you what you're good at, but only you can define what makes you tick. And don't think just because you're good at something, that makes it your purpose. I may be great at debating, but I promise you I'd make a horrible attorney.

2. **Your purpose will evolve over time.** As you grow personally and professionally, your purpose will evolve. I don't believe we're born with just one "fixed" purpose. I think we have many purposes, depending on the role we're playing and point where we are in life. Identify what your purpose is and from where your fulfillment comes, in personal, business, mental, physical, and spiritual aspects of life. Then consider how you can focus on them.

3. **You will be eminently qualified to fulfill your purpose.** Your purpose comes from your unique, personal experiences and no one has ever seen and experienced the world through your eyes. Everything about you has evolved and morphed over time as a result of your environment and experiences.

4. **Your purpose will be perfectly timed.** When the time comes to reveal and experience your purpose, you'll be perfectly prepared. Until it's unveiled, capitalize on your learning and experiences, as you're in the training ground. Consider it your own personal cocoon, and get ready because, when the time comes, you'll be able to fly!

5. **Your purpose will capitalize on your gifts and talents.** Your gifts and talents are unique to you, and identifying

and acting on them will help you determine your purpose. It's more than your skills, it's what you yearn to do. It's whatever fulfills your soul and where you operate in your strengths.

6. **You'll know your purpose when you feel it.** When you're operating in your purpose, it generates a feeling that's hard to describe—but you'll know it. Psychologists call it flow, athletes call it their zone, and it's your sweet spot, where time seems to stand still.

7. **Your purpose will help you connect to the meaning in your life.** Knowing your purpose and walking in it will bring you immense joy, which is more than happiness. You'll experience a to-the-core peace that soothes your innermost being and completes your soul. Your spirit will feel at home when you're walking in your purpose.

CHAPTER 21

Stillness in the Chaos

Do not wait on a leader... look in the mirror, it's you!
~ KATHERINE MIRACLE

Life's harried pace is often draining and the days fly by. Living in your purpose will enable you to walk confidently in being the person you were intended to be. Here are some simple ways to add meaning to your daily life, which will connect you to your purpose.

1. Find Time for Yourself

Life can be over-scheduled, which takes a toll on your mind and body. It's imperative to take care of yourself, especially when taking care of others (remember in chapter 1 where we talked about how your personal time is usually what gets the shaft when it comes to the schedule?). Think of it this way: when cars are out of gas they won't go, no matter how hard you turn the key. You're no different; you can't take care of others on a depleted tank. Your quality time for yourself is more about just that—ensuring that it's quality.

What helps you relax? What rejuvenates you? You may prefer to spend a few minutes every morning or evening quieting your mind through stretching, praying, or meditating. Or you may choose to read a book, take time to exercise, be still in nature, or journal. Whatever you do, make sure to find time for yourself throughout every day.

2. Reconnect with Your Passion

What do you yearn to do? When you were younger, did you enjoy painting, sports, dancing, or writing? Have you always wanted to travel, learn to quilt, or take a photography class? It's important to identify the activities that most fill your cup, so you can continue to take on the world. This is not a suggestion to quit your day job and start a new business with your passions, because then your passions become work. This is about reconnecting with what inspires and recharges you.

Personally, I've always wanted to learn to paint. I keep telling myself, "When I retire in 20 years, I'll take a class." Why on earth should I wait? And with my health history and track record, who's to say I'll even make it that long!? Don't delay prioritizing yourself. Whether it's gardening, cooking, sewing, photography, salsa dancing, or yoga, make time for you and what you enjoy doing, as opposed to just going where you're pulled. Dedicating at least one to two hours a week will make you feel more grounded, more connected, more centered.

3. Be Authentic

Do you have friends or family members who know you? The real you? How genuine are you in your relationships? I'm not encouraging you to bare your soul to the Starbucks barista, but have some people you're transparent with and invested in, who you can count on to be honest with you. True authenticity takes courage, but leaves us feeling more wholehearted. Surround yourself with people who love you for you, in spite of your faults, flaws, or past mistakes. Have people in your life with whom you don't have to wear the mask of perfection.

Although it's tempting to fill our friend bucket with people who approve of and validate us, make sure you aren't surrounding yourself with yes-people. True friends will say the hard stuff, when it's needed to support you and see you grow.

Also, are you being a true friend? This doesn't give you permission to be rude or hateful, but speak the truth in love. Be genuine, thoughtful, and authentic in your relationships and it'll be easier to get that in return.

4. Volunteer

Setting time aside to give back of yourself to those less fortunate is a great way to find deeper meaning in life. Many times you can find such opportunities through your employer, religious center, or even find volunteer opportunities online. Non-profit organizations would be thrilled to have your expertise and knowledge, and typically volunteers are the heart of their organization. Whatever you choose to do, whether it's spending time helping a local food pantry, reading at your children's school, serving on a non-profit board, or participating in mission work overseas, volunteering is a way to help you get connected to the world around you.

5. Be a Spokesperson for Your Beliefs

What ignites your passion and creativity? It may be helping others in need, environmental issues, or even helping others strategize and problem solve. Whatever you stand for, whatever your beliefs, use it as a chance to connect with others to find common ground. In our 21st century society we have so many modern conveniences to give us shortcuts—there's an app for everything in our microwave lives. What we tend to lack is a true human connection and a passion that connects us to others.

I'm passionate about a lot of things in my life and anyone

who knows me is aware of what has ignited my internal fires. My biggest passion, and what I know to be my purpose in life, is helping others see their worth and value. I've had the privilege of going to Zambia twice with my family and teaching vacation Bible school to orphaned children. I've never experienced such a feeling of complete wholeness—a feeling I can't describe—as I did when I spent time investing in those children. They lacked in every earthly material possession, even food, but they were hopeful, some even joyful, and eager for life. They were too young to have identified their purpose yet, but they were filled with the knowledge they were created for a reason.

I've also been overseas and taught English to college-aged students, which was a completely different experience. What was most concerning to me there was their lack of hope in finding their purpose. They asked me where my hope was and I shared that it was only through my faith in God, who, for me is Jesus, that I was able to find and connect to my passions, purpose, and hope. I've thought of those young adults many, many times over the years and wondered how they were doing. I pray they found their purpose and were confident in the fact that they had a greater role in life to fill than what they believed.

6. Move Forward

Life is a journey of transformation to be your personal best—regardless of others. What I've found is confidence is only developed in the face of hard times. Only through resilience and perseverance can we ever find our true, best selves—which, ultimately, is where our confidence lies. Every time you take a risk, knowing that you may not succeed, you add to your confidence reserves.

Every time you stand up for someone being treated unfairly at work, you add to your confidence inventory. Every time you stare fear in the eyes and say, "Get behind me, fear; I got this!" and move forth in spite of the feeling, you're building your stockpile of confidence that you can access whenever you want! You own it; no one can take it away because you earned it.

Along with courage, confidence is revealed when you have faith to identify your purpose. Your purpose is as unique, and important, to living fully as is your DNA. Faith is what you need to dig down deep to identify your purpose, through self-reflection and asking yourself some hard questions. You can't find your purpose from your parents, a book, a boss, or a spouse—they may help affirm your journey, but ultimately you have to find it from within yourself.

CONCLUSION

The Future Is Ours

Life is not easy for any of us. But what of that? We must have perseverance and above all confidence in ourselves. We must believe that we are gifted for something and that this thing must be attained.

~ Marie Curie

We've come a long way and made some valiant strides in our efforts to gain gender equality in the workforce, but our climb to the top isn't over yet. As half the professional workforce is comprised of females, it would be rational to estimate that approximately half the corporate executive-level staff would be female as well. Unfortunately, that's simply nowhere near the case.

As indicated by the evidence, women comprise less than five percent of the highest paid roles—top executive positions of Fortune 500 companies. The healthcare industry is ahead of the general population, sadly, with an average of only 11 percent of women at the CEO level. That's just not enough.

We're encouraged to lean in, and I support that message, but even when we do, factors and obstacles remain. However, seeing our journey as a labyrinth, or maze, instead of an impenetrable glass ceiling, gives us hope that executive roles can be conquered—we can persevere and achieve our goal of getting to our desired position. Buying into the existence of a glass ceiling is part of what keeps us from believing in ourselves and our abilities to achieve.

When we realize we have the power to achieve corporate (or any level of) success, the outlook becomes brighter. We aren't victims to some mythical ceiling—we're more than conquerors. The journey isn't promised to be easy, but it'll be worth it. So, now that we've covered those four obstacles at length, let's recap what we know.

Family Matters

First, we discussed how juggling the needs of a family and growing a career was the challenge most often experienced, as every female with children reported this balance was a struggle. As you can see, women, we're not alone in dealing with the pressures of raising a family on our climb to the top of the corporate ladder—but we aren't alone in raising our children either. Children benefit and learn valuable life lessons from seeing you work hard, and you benefit from the experience of working.

The way you can be most successful, though, is by ensuring you have support on your team. If you're a single mom, I applaud you. You have a tough job, but don't give up. You have one of the most thankless jobs in the world and you can still build your team by surrounding yourself with supportive, encouraging friends and family.

If you're married, great—there's your co-captain. I encourage you to make your spouse your partner. Sit down together, strategize, and get a game plan (on paper) of how you can work together to make both of you successful at home and at work. I encourage you to write out all the weekly, monthly, and spur-of-the-moment household chores that need to be done. Assign them one at a time by making it a game—Red Rover style.

If your kids are old enough to work an iPad, then get them in on the assignments too. Children benefit from learning early-on about responsibilities and seeing that no one gets a free ride in life. You're not alone in the house; don't allow yourself to be alone in the responsibilities of taking care of it.

As far as that little negative voice in your head that contributes to your guilt, here's my suggestion: name her and call her out. Stop giving her power to hold you back. Do what you can to set yourself up to be successful, which may mean you outsource and collaborate with others, and that's okay. That doesn't diminish your value or effort. You're not a bad mom or a bad wife because you're resourceful—quite the contrary.

The flip side of family life is balancing workplace responsibilities. In our nonstop culture, it's easy to see work as an all-or-nothing scenario, giving us a reason to justify resigning altogether. However, completely checking out of the workforce to stay home and grow a family isn't the only solution. Part-time employment and independent contractor positions are options, as well as staying full-time and/or making efforts to change workplace policies.

However, if you work part time, be ready to commit to being all hands on deck when and if you're needed and the time comes. The key is to be the employee your employer doesn't want to lose—work hard, be solution-focused, and be a great team player.

Overall, don't look at this period of your life as final. Your children won't be little and needy forever, so don't close the door on your career when a little bit of creativity can help your family navigate through this season; your children will learn so much from you about responsibility and resilience, and those are lessons they'll draw on for the rest of their lives.

Age to Engage

The next obstacle women reported was feeling at a crossroads in their employment. We discussed how women were feeling challenged in three ways: family responsibilities (as previously mentioned), limited advancement opportunities in their current organizations, and perceived limitations as a result of their age. Many questioned what the next stage in their life would entail, wondering if they were supposed to stay in their role at their present company or branch out and try something new. The hardest move to make, though, is venturing into unchartered territory, especially when you're comfortable where you are.

What do you do when you're happy with your employer, but you want more challenge in your role—and advancement opportunities in your current organization are limited? That's a very real scenario many women mentioned. Do you stay where you are? Do you leave and hope you make the right decision? Although this situation may not seem like something specific to females, it is a limitation that affects our journeys very differently than it does a male's career ascension.

"Why?" you ask. Well, that's easy. Leadership roles become more limited as you rise through the organizational ranks. Because work life doesn't happen in a silo, women are generally getting hit at the same time trying to navigate the maze of the other three obstacles—family, gender challenges, and lack of confidence.

However, if employers want to support their key employees and help them feel more fulfilled, they need to identify what deepens their engagement in the organization. Overall, most content employees don't want to leave—but why settle for content when you can be happy? Engaged employees result in happier, more invested assets. But it's up to both parties, employer and employee, to communicate what's needed and necessary to create deeper levels of engagement.

Hit from All Sides

Gender was the third obstacle we discussed. In general, our society has ascribed certain qualities to males and females, detailing and defining how each gender is expected to behave; as a result, gender stereotypes and behavioral expectations have evolved. Women, for the most part, are supposed to act communally by being nurturing, compassionate, gentle, kind, and collaborative.

Men, on the other hand, are expected and accepted to behave in agentic ways—authoritative, assertive, ambitious, competitive, and decisive. When females behave agentically, or opposite of how they're stereotyped and predicted to act, they're met with opposition; they face a double bind. This problem is exacerbated by the fact that leadership in the working world has traditionally been aligned with masculine characteristics.

Ample amounts of leadership advice have been given to women, and we were previously encouraged to simply "act like a man" in order to advance our careers; however, these well-intentioned suggestions set us up to fail, because of the double bind. Another result, albeit inadvertent, of suggesting women behave more agentically is the false assumption that women don't innately have the ability to draw on their own strengths to lead. This starts us down the slippery slope of buying into the lie that only those with male characteristics are capable of being strong leaders.

Leadership tides are turning toward a preference for servant or transformational leaders, reflective of communal characteristics.

As more interest and research has been garnered on the subject of leadership, an intriguing trend has emerged though. Leadership tides are turning more toward a desire for a ser-

vant or transformational approach, which are both direct reflections of communal characteristics. For the most part, top-
down, "because I said so" transactional leadership models are
becoming less favored.

This is great news for women, as we tend to possess more
communal properties. But, now we have to advance to the level of executive-level leadership to show what we can accomplish and what we're made of. What's holding us back from
those positions? Fascinating question.

One reason is because of the next subject we covered—the
sad realities of the existence of the good ol' boys' club and their
impact on keeping women out of the corner office. Regardless
of your current industry, some men are not supportive of the
advancement of women into their executive turf. These good
ol' boys prefer to keep us in entry and mid-level management
positions, so we're advanced enough to have some level of
clout but not in positions of enough power where we have
significant authority.

However, as discussed, we discovered men aren't the only
guilty party in holding women back. We also saw the way
women can impede other women and how some mean girls
grow into mean women as a result of their own insecurities.
Many of the women on the road to career advancement experienced manipulation, gossip, backstabbing, and betrayal. An
outstanding number of women, approximately 80 percent, recounted how they experienced some form of harassment from
another female. That's unbelievable and troubling, ladies.

The issue and reality at stake here is that if we don't start
lifting each other up and supporting our fellow females, we'll
never achieve equality. That's significant and bears repeating.
If women don't stop seeing other women as the enemy and
sabotaging their efforts to succeed, we'll never gain equal
ground in the workforce, in pay, or in leadership positions.

If, collectively, women see other women as members of

the same team and build them up, we'd have unlimited power. When women begin to mentor and sponsor other females who aspire to follow in their leadership footprints, we'll more fully demonstrate the value we bring to the table.

Studies have already proven how women benefit organizations when they're included in the leadership landscape, but when we behave in ways that are spiteful and vindictive to others, we shoot our entire gender in the foot. Through our actions, we're responsible for closing the door to other women who could potentially help pave the way to workplace gender equality.

Being a leader and guiding teams takes the ability to gain respect and establish a good working relationship with everyone involved. Ladies, we have the power, education, drive, intelligence, and grit to do it.

Consider the leadership characteristics of great leaders you've either worked with or known (male or female) and reflect on what's made them great leaders. Aspire to work toward emulating their positive characteristics. Be the leader you'd want to work for. But first, it's going to take us getting to the real heart of the problem to be able to work together to conquer the boardroom.

The Heart of the Matter

We've overcome a lot of hurdles on our climb to the top, but there's one more obstacle remaining—ourselves. The biggest obstacle to our advancement is our lack of confidence in our own gifts, strengths, and abilities to be the leaders we were called to be. Our confidence, or lack thereof, has the power to affect all other aspects of our lives.

Confidence is found when courage and faith intersect. When you begin to have the courage to speak up, even when it's hard, for what you need and believe in—whether it be against injustices at the office, getting help around the house, raising your hand for the promotion, or standing up for your own equal pay—you let go of the power you previously gave to fear and begin to gain clarity on the power you hold. When you start to take action steps toward creating and defining the career you desire, you realize your potential is in your hands.

But confidence is not found only in having the courage to act. Courage must meet faith to gain true confidence in who you are and to walk in being the person you're meant to be. Confidence is the byproduct you achieve when you have the courage and faith to walk in your purpose. And confidence is found in knowing you have a calling and purpose in your life that belongs to you, and you alone. No one else can tell you what your purpose is or can walk in your purpose for you.

When you know and walk in alignment with your purpose, then you'll begin to see that your strengths, gifts, and abilities are independent of anyone else's, and vice versa. You'll awaken and ignite a confidence that doesn't come from anything or anyone other than you—and no one else can take it away.

Confident women lift each other up, cheer each other on, and support one another. They don't tear each other down, backstab, gossip, or gloat when others do poorly. They feel fulfilled in their own gifts and abilities, and want to see those around them fulfilled as well. They talk in ways that encourage and inspire others to do well. Their words and actions are reflective of true integrity and a sound, resolute character.

Part of what makes great leaders is the belief in themselves and their cause, and they have the courage to stand up for what they believe in during times of adversity. If you're putting on a show to lead like a man, or in a way you think is "right," and you're not leading in a style that's authentic and genuine to you, then you're not aligned with your core abilities and strengths.

But, there's good news—tomorrow is a new day. Every day you can commit to taking the next right step, and I encourage you to reflect on what you want to represent to the world. What light do you want to shine?

Your Future: Your Legacy

The world has been waiting for you to be the leader you were meant to be. It's time you step into your purpose, your strengths, and your legacy. Yes, there'll be difficult times, but whoever promised that life was going to be easy? If you picture each obstacle as a tunnel, then where does it become the most uncertain? The darkest? The most difficult to see and navigate? Yes, the middle. And so many of us turn back when we feel like we can't continue on.

We quit and run back to the familiar. We go back to the place of the known, even though we aren't fulfilled there. We settle for complacency. We get discouraged during hardship, instead of pressing on and believing in ourselves and that we're destined for more.

What we don't see, though, is that if we continue to push through to the other side, our breakthrough will be there, waiting. If we persevere, we'll see that we're made of so much more than we think and give ourselves credit for. I encourage you to make a commitment to build your resilience. Accept that things may be difficult. Yes, sometimes things will be hard. And that's okay. Know that going in and be mentally, emotionally, and physically prepared to persist. But don't let being your best be negotiable; your legacy is not optional.

Now, get out there and go conquer!

REFERENCES

American College of Healthcare Executives. (2012). *A Comparison of the career attainments of men and women healthcare executives.* Chicago, IL: ACHE.

American Psychological Association. (n.d.). *The Road to Resilience.* Retrieved from American Psychological Association: http://www.apa.org/helpcenter/road-resilience.aspx

Babcock, L., & Laschever, S. (2007). *Women don't ask: The high cost of avoiding negotiation- and positive strategies for change.* New York, NY: Bantam Dell.

Barbuto, J. E., & Gifford, G. T. (2010). Examining gender differences of servant leadership: An analysis of agentic and communal properties of the servant leadership questionnaire. *Journal of Leadership Education,* 4-19.

Barnett, R., & Hyde, J. (2001). Women, Men, Work, and Family. *American Psychologist,* 781-796.

Bass, B., & Riggio, R. E. (2006). *Transformational leadership.* Mahwah, NJ: Lawrence Erlbaum Associates.

Bernard, T. S. (2014). *For Workers, Less Flexible Companies.* Retrieved from The New York Times: http://www.nytimes.com/2014/05/20/business/for-workers-less-flexible-companies.html?_r=0

Bian, L., Leslie, S.-J., & Cimpian, A. (2017). Gender stereotypes about intellectual ability emerge early and influence children's interests. *Science,* 389-391.

Bleidorn, W., Arslan, R., Denissen, J., Rentfrow, P., Gebauer, J., Potter, J., & Gosling, S. (2016). Age and gender differences in self-esteem: A cross-cultural window. *Journal of Personality and Social Psychology,* 111(3), 396-410.

Boatwright, K. J., & Forrest, L. (2000). Leadership preferences: The influence of gender and needs for connection on workers' ideal preference for leadership behaviors. *Journal of Leadership Studies* 7(2), 18-24.

Carless, S. (1998). Gender differences in transformational leadership: An examination of superior, leader, and subordinate perspectives. *Sex Roles*, 39(11-12), 887-902.

Catalyst. (2007). *The double-bind dilemma for women in leadership: Damned if you do, doomed if you don't.* New York, NY: Catalyst.

Catalyst. (2016). *Statistical overview of women in the workforce.* Retrieved from Catalyst: http://www.catalyst.org/knowledge/statistical-overview-women-workforce

Coltrane, S. (2000). Research on household labor: Modeling and measuring social embeddedness of routine family work. *Journal of Marriage and Family,* 62(4), 1208-1233.

Cook, L. P. (2006). "Doing" gender in context: Household bargaining and risk of divorce in Germany and the United States. *American Journal of Sociology,* 112(2), 442-472.

Coontz, S. (2006). *Marriage, a history.* Penguin Books.

Coutu, D. (2002). How Resilience Works. *Harvard Business Review.*

Desvaunx, G., Devillard-Hoellinger, S., & Meaney, M. C. (2008). A business case for women. *The McKinsey Quarterly,* 4.

Development Dimensions International, Inc. (2015). *Global Leadership Forecast 2014|2015.* Retrieved from DDI World: http://www.ddiworld.com/DDI/media/trend-research/global-leadership-forecast-2014-gender-subreport_tr_ddi.pdf?ext=.pdf

Dillaway, H., & Pare, E. (2008). Locating mothers: How cultural debates about stay-at-home versus working mothers define women and home. *Journal of Family Issues,* 29(4), 437-464.

Eagly, A. H., & Carli, L. L. (2007a). *Through the labyrinth: The truth about how women become leaders.* Boston, MA: Harvard Business School Press.

Eagly, A., & Carli, L. (2007b). *Women and the labyrinth of leadership.* Retrieved from Harvard Business Review: https://hbr.org/2007/09/

women-and-the-labyrinth-of-leadership

Eaglyl, A. H., & Johannesen-Schmidt, M. C. (2001). The leadership styles of men and women. *Journal of Social Issues*, 57(4), 781-797.

Ely, R. J. (1995). The power in demography: Women's social construction of gender identity at work. *Academy of Management Journal* 38(3), 589-634.

Ely, R. J., Stone, P., & Ammerman, C. (2014). Rethink what you "know" about high-achieving women. *Harvard Business Review*.

Families and Work Institute. (2014). *2014 National Study of Employers*.

Grunspan, D., Goodreau, S. M., Eddy, S. L., Brownell, S. E., Wiggins, B. L., & Crowe, A. J. (2016). Males under-estimate academic performance of their female peers in undergraduate biology classrooms. *PLOS One*, 11(2).

Hamel, L., Firth, J., & Brodie, M. (2014). *Kaiser Famiily Foundation/ New York Times/CBS News Non-Employed Poll*. Kaiser Family Foundation.

Hancock, A. B., & Rubin, B. J. (2015). Influence of communication partner's gender on language. *Journal of language and social psychology*, 34(1), 46-64.

Hewlett, S. A., & Luce, C. B. (2005). Off-ramps and on ramps: Keeping talented women on the road to success. *Harvard Business Review* 83(3), 43-54.

Holiday, E., & Rosenberg, J. (2009). *Mean Girls, Meaner Women*. LaVergne, TN: Orchid Press.

Kay, K., & Shipman, C. (2014). *The Confidence Code*. New York, NY: Harper Collins.

Lepore, M. (2014). *Mean girls at work: Why women are bullies*. Retrieved from Levo: http://www.levo.com/articles/career-advice/ mean-girls-at-work

Luthans, F. (2002). The need for and meaning of positive organizational behavior. *Journal of Organizational Behavior*, 695-706.

MacMillan, A. (2016). *Fox News Health*. Retrieved from Fox News: http://www.foxnews.com/health/2016/08/25/women-thrive-as-prima-ry-breadwinner-while-men-suffer-study-finds.html

McDonagh, K. J., & Paris, N. M. (2013). The leadership labyrinth: Leveraging the talents of women to transform health care. *Nursing Administration Quarterly*, 6-12.

McKinsey & Company. (2015a). *Moving women to the top: McKinsey global survey results*. Retrieved from http://www.mckinsey.com/insights/organization/moving_women_to_the_top_mckinsey_glob-al_survey_results

McKinsey & Company. (2015b). *Women in the workplace*. Retrieved from Women in the workplace: http://womenintheworkplace.com/ui/pdfs/Women_in_the_Workplace_2015.pdf?v=5

Meers, S., & Strober, J. (2009). *Getting to 50/50: How working couples can have it all by sharing it all*. New York: Bantam.

Milkie, M. A., Raley, S. B., & Bianchi, S. M. (2009). Taking the second shift: Time allocations and time pressures of U.S. parents with pre-schoolers. *Social Forces*, 88(2), 487-517.

Miller, C. C. (2014). *Even among Harvard graduates, women fall short of their work expectations*. Retrieved from The New York Times: https://www.nytimes.com/2014/11/30/upshot/even-among-harvard-graduates-women-fall-short-of-their-work-expectations.html

Moss-Racusin, C. A., Dovidio, J. F., Brescoll, V. L., Graham, M. J., & Handelsman, J. (2012). Science faculty's subtle gender biases favor male students. *Proceedings of the National Academy of Sciences of the United States of America*, 109(41), 16474-16479.

Perry, M. (2015). *Women earned majority of doctoral degrees in 2014 for 6th straight year, and outnumber men in grad school 136 to 100*. Retrieved from AEIdeas: https://www.aei.org/publication/women-earned-majority-of-doctoral-degrees-in-2014-for-6th-straight-year-and-outnumber-men-in-grad-school-136-to-100/

Pershing. (2016). *Americans crave a new kind of leader - and women are ready to deliver*. Retrieved from Pershing: https://www.pershing.com/our-thinking/thought-leadership/americans-crave-a-new-kind-of-leader-and-women-are-ready-to-deliver

Rezvani, S. (2010). *The next generation of women leaders: What you need to lead but won't learn in business school.* Santa Barbara, CA: ABC-CLIO, LLC.

Rezvani, S. (2012). *Mean girls at work.* Retrieved from *The Washington Post*: https://www.washingtonpost.com/national/on-leadership/mean-girls-at-work/2012/01/24/gIQAu4suNQ_story.html

Schein, V. (2001). A global look at psychological barriers to women's progress in management. *Journal of Social Issues* 57(4), 675-688.

Stein, J. (2013). *Millennials: The me me me generation.* Retrieved from *Time*: http://time.com/247/millennials-the-me-me-me-generation/

Steinpreis, R. E., Anders, K. A., & Ritzke, D. (1999). The impact of gender on the review of curricula vitae of job applicants and tenure candidates: A national empirical study. *Sex Roles,* 509-528.

Stone, P. (2007). *Opting out? Why women really quit careers and head home.* Berkeley, CA: University of California Press.

Turner, C. (2014). *Gender and generational differences: The intersection.* Retrieved from *The Huffington Post*: http://www.huffingtonpost.com/caroline-turner/gender-and-generational-d_b_5974624.html

U.S. Census Bureau. (2013). *Table FG2. Married Couple Family Groups, by Family Income, and Labor Force Status of Both Spouses: 2013.* Retrieved from U.S. Census Bureau: http://www.census.gov/hhes/families/data/cps2013FG.html

U.S. Census Bureau. (2015). *F10- Family Groups.* Retrieved from U.S. Census Bureau: http://www.census.gov/hhes/families/data/cps-2015FG.html

U.S. Department of Labor, Bureau of Labor Statistics. (2015). *Table 11: Employed persons by detailed occupation, sex, race, and Hispanic or Latino ethnicity.* Retrieved from Current population survey: https://www.bls.gov/cps/tables.htm#empstat

Wallace, K. (2015). *5 ways women can stop tearing each other down at work.* Retrieved from CNN: http://www.cnn.com/2015/03/25/living/

feat-women-helping-women-sophia-nelson/

Walsh, M. W. (2001). So where are the corporate husbands? For women at the top, something is missing: Social, wifely support. *The New York Times*. Retrieved from http://www.nytimes.com

Warner, J. (2014). *Fact Sheet: The Women's Leadership Gap*. Retrieved from Center for American Progress: https://www.americanprogress.org/issues/women/reports/2014/03/07/85457/fact-sheet-the-womens-leadership-gap/

Webster's Dictionary. (n.d.). *Confidence*. Retrieved from Webster's Dictionary: http://www.webster-dictionary.net/definition/confidence

Weil, P., & Mattis, M. (2001). Narrowing the gender gap in healthcare management. *Healthcare Executive*, 12-17.

Winograd, M., & Hais, M. D. (2013). *Race? No, millennials care most about gender equality*. Retrieved from The Atlantic: http://www.theatlantic.com/politics/archive/2013/10/race-no-millennials-care-most-about-gender-equality/430305/

Workplace Bullying Institute. (2014). *Workplace bullying: Gender and the U.S. bullying experience*. Retrieved from Workplace bullying: http://www.workplacebullying.org/2014-gender/